Cover Design by Erikka Yvonne

Cover Photography by Bre'Ann White

Book Production Management by BM Webster Publishing

With contributions by Blake Benberry, Taylor Harrell, Chigozie

Uwazurike, Meagan Ward, Loren Entsuah, Lance Woods, Jade Ulmer, Bee Brown, Toni Jones, Erin A. White, Klaudia Jakubiak, and Ingrid

Ellis.

For more information about scheduling the author for speaking engagements, or book discounts please contact the author at

hello@danielledhughes.com.

www.amybbook.com

www.danielledhughes.com

Dedication

This book is dedicated to the legacy of my Grandfather, David Jackson, Jr.

Thank you for being the best example of a God-fearing provider, hardworking entrepreneur and constantly investing in the education of your family and your community.

In memory of my Grandfather, or "Papa" as I affectionately called him, a portion of each book sold will go towards the David Jackson Jr. Scholarship for Emerging Leaders. These funds will support young people in their scholastic and entrepreneurial endeavors.

Thank you, Papa for leading the way. I'm honored to be a part of your legacy. I hope I'm making you proud.

To Shanel and Destani, your time on earth may have been short, but the impact that you had on so many is everlasting. You both left a lasting impression on me and I am forever grateful for the time we spent together. I hope to live my life as boldly and fearlessly as you both did. Fly high, ladies. Forever in my heart.

Acknowledgements

I'd like to take the time to thank every single person who made this book a reality. If you have been a part of my life in any way, shape or form – this is for you.

To my Mama: If I told you that I wanted to build an aircraft and fly to space today you would ask me how much it costs to get to outer space so you can come visit. Ha! Thank you for encouraging me, thank you for believing in me, thank you for taking care of me and supporting everything that I've ever done. I don't know where I would be without you.

To my Dad, Mr. Rob, My Granny, My Nana and John, My little sis Lauren and all of the rest of my siblings, my Aunts and Uncles, cousins, sister-friends, framily (friends that have turned into family), My amazing TFP fam and everyone in between – THANK YOU! Each of you have played integral roles in my journey and I'll never be able to thank you enough.

To every teacher, mentor, coach, professor and employer (even the ones who fired me!) thank you for seeing something in me that I didn't see in myself. You all took a chance on me – and whether it worked out or not – it made me a better person and your mentorship and love along the way has been invaluable.

To my little ones: Blake, Grayson, Brayden and my Goddaughter Aria – I hope that you four know that the sky is the limit and you can do absolutely anything that you put your mind to. This was created for you. When you're older, I hope that you'll use the principles shared in this book to create a life that you're proud of. I love you!

To Brittney Webster, the woman behind BM Webster Publishing who made this book come to life, and Erikka Simpson who created the amazing book design: WE DID IT!! Thank you for answering all of my questions, hyping me up and most importantly – holding me accountable to finish writing. It's been a long time coming and it wouldn't have happened without you two. Thank you!

To every dreamer, doer, misfit, every person who has been told NO more than YES. The changemakers, the bosses, the optimists, the realists, the ones who strive to be just a bit better than the day before – this one's for you.

Cheers to making your bed!

-DH

Table of Contents

Foreword

The first day of school generates excitement for teachers and students alike. Fortunately for me, I was able to experience that special exhilaration 35 times during my teaching career. I was also able to see the first day through the lens of parochial, private and public schools, from special and regular education perspectives, in both urban and suburban settings and I saw children from all parts of the socioeconomic spectrum.

Looking out at a sea of student faces, I would often wonder which students would stand out and why? Would our time together go beyond the school year? Would we meet again later in life? As I asked these questions, I'd wonder what were the young scholars thinking and what questions were they asking? In life, sometimes answers present themselves in profound ways. Danielle Denise Hughes was one particular student of mine who would do just that.

I met Danielle as her sixth-grade language arts teacher. As fate would have it, years later, at a graduation celebration with many proud parents and former students present our paths intersected again. Seeing and reconnecting with her would be another of life's greatest pleasures that has led to this foreword for **Always Make Your Bed.**

As Danielle and I have become reacquainted and I've read **AMYB,** I am struck that the 11-year-old burgeoning reader, writer and eager problem solver that I met years ago has blossomed into an effervescent student of life filled with passion and drive. So, it comes as no surprise to see this capable young woman write a cleverly structured multi-genre, practical 'how to', self-help, autobiographical memoir.

There are many facets and lessons to be learned from **AMYB.** Reading and working though the text will take you on a journey of self-discovery. Its honest author will provide fitting biblical quotes for the faith filled reader, blank spaces for ideas, note taking and planning that will assist in the implementation of concepts that the reader will want to pursue.

Danielle's story will come to life as she shares learning experiences both triumphant and challenging. Ready yourself for this very worthwhile ride that will definitely lay the groundwork for a new and successful you. Make the commitment to **AMYB,** you'll be grateful for putting forth the effort that will ensure that your goals will be achieved. Without further ado, I'd like to present to you... ***Always Make Your Bed***

-Kathleen Hayes-Parvin

Danielle's (happily retired) 6th Grade English Teacher turned Mentor

Introduction

I graduated from high school with a 1.9 GPA. I was probably the least likely to succeed out of my graduating class.

Since then, I've made the Forbes list, traveled across the world sharing my story with crowds of thousands, authored a book, and some other pretty cool stuff in between.

How did I manage to turn my life around you may ask?

I always make my bed.

I'm sure you're wondering what does making your bed have to do with anything, right? Well, I'll tell you. To become successful, you must remain consistent.

I haven't always been the best at staying consistent. So much so, that I decided to choose one thing that I KNEW I could get done each day. Thus, I began praying and making my bed every morning. Sometimes those are the only things that get done in a day, but it's a task checked off of my to-do list, nonetheless.

Consistency breeds consistency. Once I began making my bed on a regular basis, I started to create a steady routine for the rest of my life as well. In the words of Myleik Teele; "I believe that being consistent in just one thing per day will bleed into other areas of our lives."

While you're navigating the pages of this book, I hope you'll laugh, but most importantly I hope you'll learn. Learn from the mistakes that I've made and realize that you truly have the power to create your own destiny. I always knew that God had a plan for me. I never understood it then. I get it now.

If you're struggling to figure out what it is that you've been destined to do, my biggest piece of advice is to keep trusting God and your journey. As you'll find out in the pages of this book, HIS plans are always greater than ours.

Stay consistent, take care of yourself and others, and keep your dreams larger than life.

Most importantly…

Always, always, always make your bed.

Enjoy!

Xoxo,

-DH

PRINCIPLE: I

"Write the vision; make it plain."

- Habakkuk 2:2

"THE FORBES LIST?!?" I shrieked in total disbelief as I nervously maneuvered out of my driver seat and bolted down the street. Me? On the Forbes list? HOW SWAY?! As I slowly came back to my senses, I realized it wasn't a dream. Had all of my hard work really paid off? Like this?

***

The day was November 14th, 2017. Nothing was unusual about this day. Little did I know, it would be the day that changed my life forever. I woke up with the intention that this day would be just like any other. I went through my regular morning routine which consisted of praying, showering, and eating. I then swiftly hopped in my car and remembered that my engine light had been on for weeks... literally weeks. Don't try that at home, kids.

I'd had enough of hearing the annoying "ding" alerting me that my car was wayyyy overdue for an oil change seeping through my car stereo. So, I decided that would be the day that I made my way to Valvoline to get a dreaded oil change. Thinking back - as normal as this day seemed, I guess I knew in my heart that something was different. As I slowly released my sunroof to let the crisp fall breeze slip in, I casually rotated the dial on my radio until I heard Charlamagne Tha God's voice on The Breakfast Club. Instead of deeming someone "Donkey of the Day" he was sharing a story of how practicing gratitude changed his life. This particular segment caught my attention because gratitude is something that I had been exceptionally intentional about that year. I made a mental note of his anecdote and continued to pull into the lot of Valvoline. As I drove my SUV onto the bay to park, I decided to scroll through the Forbes Under 30 list that had been released just a few hours before. What happened next was beyond shocking. It was incredibly life-changing in the most exhilarating of ways.

As I scrolled through the categories in admiration, I landed at the Education category. To my surprise, my name and photo were listed as an honoree. Wow! Needless to say, I hopped out of my car mid-oil change and ran down the street screaming.

***

You see, this specific honor is one that I had been striving for since October of 2014 when I created my very first vision board. I created that board as a flat broke, stressed, and depressed college grad with no job leads in sight. I promised myself that I would never end up back in Detroit after college… and yet there I was. Back in Detroit, back in my Mom's house, and back in my childhood room where the B2K and Lil' Bow Wow posters were still plastered to the walls. I had recently graduated with my Bachelor's in Telecommunications and applied to 56 jobs in news. Yep, you read that right. Fifty-six. You see, since the age of 16, it had been my dream to have a career as a news anchor. I made sure that I applied for every internship and externship, and job shadowed everyone I possibly could to turn this dream into a reality. Yet, here I was: 22 and jobless. (Well, that's partially because I had also been recently fired from a law office.) Firing will be a common theme throughout this book. Stay tuned. I was just about at the end of my rope and indulged in pints of Ben and Jerry's ice cream nightly to suppress my pain. *Sigh*

It's rare that I say something changed my life because I can tend to be a bit skeptical at times, but my vision board most certainly did. I can recall expressing to two of my good friends how quickly I felt myself tumbling into a downward spiral. As true friends do, they swore they had the perfect remedy to help me forget all about it.

"Let's make vision boards…"

It was in that moment that my reality as I knew it changed. Since I was just so fed up with the current trajectory of my life, I knew that cutting pictures out of magazines would no longer suffice. I couldn't make just any ol' vision board. I knew deep down that if I wanted to see change, I needed to be intentional. I went straight to my notebook and made a list of 30 things that I wanted to see happen in my life within the next 5 years. Little did I know; I was practicing the law of attraction and didn't even know it. I made my list, aggressively snatched it out of my notebook, and went straight to Google to find photos to accompany them.

PRO TIP !

When creating vision boards or setting goals for yourself, be as SPECIFIC and INTENTIONAL as possible. You want to make an extra $20,000 this year? Don't post a dollar bill to your vision board. You're telling the Universe that all you want is a dollar. Write yourself a check (yes, write a check out to yourself and sign it!) for the exact amount that you want to manifest. Then post it to a mirror or someplace that you're forced to look everyday. Start working towards it and watch what happens.

BEST PRACTICES FOR CREATING A VISION BOARD:

- Make a list of 20 things that you would like to see happen in your life in the next year, the next 5 years, or the next 10 years.

- Don't rely on magazines to describe your vision for you. Take to the internet and create a Pinterest board or Google document that depicts your vision with photos from Google images.

- Add motivational quotes and affirmations that represent how you want to feel.

- Don't use flimsy, oversized, paper boards. I prefer using Styrofoam because it's sturdier and lasts much longer. You can even use cardstock and frame it. (I especially enjoy the ones from the Dollar Store.) They're cheap and they work!

- Once again – be SPECIFIC. You're specific when ordering a meal at a restaurant, right? Cooked medium well, no onion, extra sauce on the side, etc… I need you to be that specific while setting goals for yourself.

A QUICK NOTE ON MAKING YOUR MOST EFFECTIVE VISION BOARDS: You have to actually SEE the things that you want to happen in your life before they manifest in the physical form. It is a must that you train your mind to believe that what you want actually exists and that it is on its way to you at any moment. You have to be able to see yourself launching that business, finding your soulmate (make a list of all of the qualities you're looking for and believe that person is somewhere looking for you), finishing school, becoming a homeowner, or whatever it is that your heart desires. If you don't see it, how do you expect

₌ to come to fruition? Always keep your thoughts aligned with your goals.

***

Hours had gone by, and I was still staring at my laptop while typing like a mad woman. I created a Google collage of what my next 5 years was going to look like. I started by printing photos of a news station, an ABC news logo, and two Forbes magazines with powerful women on the cover. I also printed a photo of myself and my business partners with a rough draft of our logo, a 501c3 stamp, and a debit card which would represent our business account.

At the time of this writing, I have been featured in not one but TWO Forbes magazines. Look at GOD! I don't say any of this to brag or boast, but to let you know that it can and *will* happen for you, too. If I would've been able to foreshadow all of this 4 years ago, maybe I wouldn't have been so fervent and passionate about chasing a dream that only I could see. I knew I would be successful; I just never knew how or when it would happen.

Back to the vision boards. I'd finally completed my Google copy and paste masterpiece after two hours of feverish quote clipping, meticulous gluing, and strategic placement of photos to a white Styrofoam board.

"Ahhh…" I let out a sigh of satisfaction as I proudly held the board in front of my face. I felt accomplished. I felt successful. Truthfully, this was the first time I'd felt that way in a long time. I knew I wanted to make this a permanent feeling and that I would do whatever was necessary to make sure I did.

I placed my shiny new vision board on my nightstand and waited. Yup, literally waited. I just knew that once I put everything down on paper that all of these things happen for me overnight. Right?! After all, scripture says, "Do not be anxious about anything, but in every situation, by prayer and petition, with thanksgiving, present your requests to God." (Phil. 4:6) Hadn't I just done that? Yet, still – no progress. No major strides. I couldn't help but to ask myself, "What am I doing wrong?!" Well, I'll tell you exactly what I was doing wrong...

PRO TIP 2

Never ask God to order your steps if you're not willing to move your feet. I repeat... NEVER ASK GOD TO ORDER YOUR STEPS IF YOU'RE NOT WILLING TO MOVE YOUR FEET! Get it? Good.

I see this happen with people all the time. You pray for a better paying position, a better relationship, to lose weight, get picked for the Price is Right, or whatever else your heart desires... but are you actively working towards making it happen? Are you taking the necessary steps to turn this dream into a reality? If not, it's time to take an inventory of your daily habits and modify them to support your dream lifestyle. In other words: Get -To - Work. You know what you need to do, and procrastinating isn't going to make things happen for you any faster. It's okay to take it a step at a time but be sure to get it done! Slow motion is better than no mo-

tion. **Good things don't come to those who wait, they come to those who WORK.**

Once I came to my senses and realized that none of these high aspirations were going to work unless I did, I started putting strategic plans into motion. Successful people are strategic. Do you think Diddy amassed his fortune by luck or favor alone? Absolutely not. He put a strategy in place and executed. Not just one strategy, though. Several. Consistently. I **consistently** worked at every single thing I placed on my vision board for the next 30 days. I started by applying to just about every ABC affiliate news station that I could think of. Next, my partners and I actively drafted programming for our organization, and I started shopping around to dealerships for my dream car. Basically, I backed up my faith with actions and got to work. I applied to a total of 56 news stations altogether before I received one phone call. The victory call came from an ABC station (see how the law of attraction works?!) in Dothan, Alabama. A college friend of mine was working at the station and passed my name along to the news director! (I have an entire chapter on networking and relationships. We'll get to that later.) To make a long story short, I ended up being hired at that very station a little over a month after making my vision board. Preparation met perfect timing, and after MONTHS of waiting, I was well on my way... or so I thought.

PRO TIP 3

If you want to be successful, you MUST be consistent. There is absolutely no way around it. In the words of one of my 'mentors in my head' Myleik Teele:

"I believe that being consistent in just one thing per day will bleed into other areas of our lives. If you're struggling with finding the time to be consistent, take a look at your daily routine and find where you can be consistent in just one area per day."

Personally, I like to start off my mornings by praying and making my bed. *hint, hint* I have found that committing to these two practices everyday leads me to become more consistent with my spirituality, my loved ones, and my businesses.

HER STORY: Blake Benberry, Founder of The Makonnen Agency

I've been a storyteller since I learned my first words; discovered the power of the pen the moment my parents bought me my first journal. Raised by a family of natural orators which involved constant conversation and required speech-giving on birthdays, the skillset was served on a silver platter. I ate it up. Every aspect and immersive feeling from listening to stories, delivering stories and writing stories, simply made sense.

23 days into my freshly signed 3-year contract as the newest weekend anchor of a top 50 station, and life wasn't making much sense at all. Years to earn that spot and yet, that day would be my last. Honored to have parents who embrace first and ask questions later, they unhesitatingly told me to wipe my tears, hold my head up, and leave without looking back. They are my world.

So, I left. With no plan. No job. Harboring plenty guilt and shame, but with enough courage to catch a one-way flight to New York to let go of it all. Journal in hand, I was determined to become the storyteller I needed to be for no one else but me.

Once settled into the Bedstuy brownstone I would call home for a year, I did look back, on my life and my career as a journalist up until that point. It was the only way I could move forward. I reflected on the invaluable moments, lessons, and growth from my beginnings as an eager intern who evolved into morning news anchor in the small town of Dothan, Alabama, sharing stories of groundbreaking change, joy, and tragedy. Mostly tragedy. It's simply the nature of the business, and I eventually accepted that it would never be my style. One of several emerging one-man-band reporters vying for recognition, I found a friend to endure the highs and lows within that unfamiliar territory--the author of this book, whose been a sister ever since. Of all times and all places, Danielle and I were united in that small town for reasons we both have grown to understand and appreciate.

It was in my reporting reel that I would spend months editing for perfection, looking back to remember the stories that filled me in immeasurable ways and the others that left me drained and depleted. I looked back through the pages of my journals to read my most vulnerable and honest thoughts while evolving as a journalist and woman on my own for the first time in life. So many ideas were brewing. Many of which had taken a back seat to my all-consuming job. I had plans to help more people share their personal journeys and stories with the world. If only I could do so in a way that wasn't suffocating me in the process.

Of all the stories I helped share for others whether for work or without hesitation when a friend or relative was in need, it was the act of guiding others in telling their story that was the most gratifying. Providing the words when others simply didn't know how to say what they felt confirmed my most invigorating memories. I discovered my purpose, and I needed to learn how to walk in it.

I became my first client. I couldn't write the vision for any kind of storytelling business without owning my story. May be easy for some, but as they say doctors make the worst patients. I, as a journalist, was overwhelmingly uncomfortable having the questions directed at me. I dug deep into interviewing myself anyway, conjuring up good feelings and not so good, working with the facts as I was conditioned to, and honoring the first journalism code of ethics: seek the truth. Of course, the answer was within.

It's taken time to become unapologetic and proud about my career change and decisions. It was difficult letting go of others' opinions and focusing on what brings me peace because well, people's thoughts of me meant something for a long time. I am still learning not to give away that power. It's a process. However, I have learned to give power to what does matter and secure my peace by any means necessary. I hope you do too.

I learned to turn my complaints about the limitations I faced in my career into action. When I grew tired of relentlessly trying to incorporate my voice into the close-minded newsrooms, I poured that energy into my own platform. I've been blossoming ever since.

We truly can overcome any set of hindrances by creating the vision we see for ourselves. When there is no job description that fits you, write your own.

There's power in the pen. My journal served as not only a reflection of who I am and my deepest desires in life but was pivotal during my transition. Even today, it continues to be my confidant. In it, I am able to share every vulnerable thought, creative idea, hope, dream, and prayer. I take it everywhere so that no game changing idea is forgotten. Most importantly, I hold it close so that I never forget why I do what I do. My journal will always hold me accountable for what I think to be possible because what I write, I manifest.

Owning my story is the greatest gift I gave to myself. I've learned there is truly no room for a double life. Personal morals, values, and desires should never be sacrificed for professional success. Authenticity always wins the race.

By owning my story, I've become a stronger and more compassionate storyteller. I choose to share the stories of only those who speak their truths and are willing to be honest about their own. Not everyone is prepared for that kind of ingenuity. I wasn't always, and that is okay. In seeking the truth about my life and life itself, I know that true empowerment is possible when we use our words wisely and own our stories unapologetically. Only then is manifesting the vision inevitable.

IG: @BlakeBenberry I www.makonnen.agency

Think about it, what do Madam CJ Walker, Martin Luther King, and Oprah all have in common? Despite the obvious, they've all created grandiose visions for their lives, and we can all look at how it manifested for them. Oprah said it best, "Create the highest, grandest vision possible for your life, because you become what you believe."

Remember the show "*Behind the Music*?!" Well, when I was younger, I just knew that I would be profiled on that show one day. I cannot sing a lick, but my 8-year-old self was determined to make it big and land myself a spot on that show. I would daydream of having a camera crew follow me around as I showed them the ins and outs of my daily grind. I even told my mom that she should get her talking points together juuuust in case they contacted her for an interview. They never contacted her for an interview, and I never made it to the show. (Thank God!) Although it didn't work out like I had envisioned, that was my first experience with creating an extravagant vision for my life. I knew what I wanted, and I decided that it already happened. I believe that the key to seeing things manifest in your life is deciding that they've already happened no matter the circumstance. Make your requests known unto God and do the work to align with the Universe.

PRO TIP 4

Create a GRAND vision for your life. I've always thought big, and in turn I received big. I can't stress enough how important it is to set goals for yourself that are "two sizes too big" so you can GROW into them. Thinking BIG got Bill Gates to where he is today, and I'm certain it can get you where you need to be too. Write the vision. STICK to the vision no matter how hard it gets. Get around good people, give good energy, and watch what happens. If you can dream it, you can most definitely do it. I'm a witness.

Fun Fact: The day I was born, my parents brought me home from Sinai-Grace Hospital in a limo. I don't think I realized how integral (or hilarious) that was until lately. I believe that moment -- even if I was too young to remember -- planted a seed of possibility in me, which is to always dream bigger than life. Always believe that you are bigger than your current circumstances and that your life can change in just one day. The power of the mind is real, and if you change your thoughts, you will change your life. Train your mind to think just a little bigger each day. Since we're on the topic of creating visions, let me remind you of the childlike vision that's still inside of you today. Growing up, did you ever have an imaginary friend? If not, I'm sure I had enough for the both of us. I had an imaginary grandma named "Grandma Ke Ke." My Grandma Ke Ke lived in a tropical pink hut in a rainforest in Jamaica. I'm not sure how she came about, but I vividly remember going to visit her and how she'd feed me authentic Jamaican cuisine **(by the way, I've never been to Jamaica, just an important note on how extensive your imagination can be.)** Fortunately, I still use that same childlike innocence and instinct to create over the top "two sizes too big" goals for myself. Do they scare me? Yes. Do I still make them happen? Yes. Feel the fear and do it anyway. Whatever you do, make a commitment to yourself that you're going to give your all to making your dreams come to pass. You deserve it.

HER STORY: Taylor Harrell, Political Activist, Founder of Millennial Women Lead

Alexa, play The Vision by Patrick Love.

I recently just ran for office in the city of Detroit and lost. Going in to the election I was very confident. I thought I had a good chance of winning, and I did, but there were other factors in play. Campaigns cost a lot of money. To run city-wide, you easily need about 500k, and I didn't have anywhere near that much money. While I knew I wasn't going to get it, I couldn't just give up either because I'd prayed for this.

The position I was running for (the Charter Commission,) allotted for 9 seats. There were 16 people running, so I knew I had to do better than 7 of them.

I've ran successful campaigns for others in the past. One of which was for a city-council member and another for a woman who just made history in the state of Michigan by being the first Asian American woman elected to the Michigan State Senate. I knew what I was doing. I knew I needed a solid field plan. I knew how many doors to knock on, and I knew that I needed support from other elected officials because I didn't have the name ID necessary to win a race in city with over a half-million people.

I came in at number 12, garnishing 38,738 votes. I was extremely disappointed. I cried, cussed, and was dang near ready to go to jail because I felt robbed. After my emotions ran their course and I had my pity party, I learned that though the numbers said I lost, internally I gained. I grew from my experiences. I gained new friends. People respect me more. I was the youngest person in the race, but I was equipped to compete with people who have been in government longer than I've been alive.

Understand that it is up to you to choose happiness and choose to live your best life, despite whatever mishaps you encounter.

I've never been one of those people who believed in the idea that if we want to make God laugh then tell him our plans. I believe quite the opposite. I hate to get "spiritual", but I was raised in the church.

The Bible says in Habakkuk 2:2, "Write the vision; make it plain on tablets, so he may run who reads it."

A close friend of mine moved to Michigan from Virginia in the same summer that she graduated from college. Her uncle told her that she could move in with him and live rent free once she graduated, explore the job market, and gracefully grow into adulthood.

She applied for a job in the city, received an email for an interview date, and packed up her car and drove here. Talk about being bold! This girl moved all the way to Detroit without a job. With just an interview date, she told herself she was going to get the job.

And she did.

She wrote her vision.

Understand that your journey won't look like your mom, dad, brother, or sister's even though you both may be pursuing the same thing. Understand that you are not that next Michelle or Barack Obama, but you're the first you. There's power in being you and owning who you are.

To those of you still trying to navigate through life, that's okay too. You'll figure it out. Understand that what is for you will never pass you. In one of my favorite Meek Mill songs, "Wins & Losses" he says, "Wins and losses come with being bosses, so if you fall never stay down."

Failure, fallouts, and frustrations are apart of life. So, if and when you experience them, it doesn't mean that you're on the wrong path per say. Those setbacks exist to help us grow. When we get to where it is we want to go, we can reach back and let those behind us know that we've been there, and that they can always *write their vision.*

IG: @TaylorHarrell I www.taylorharrell.com

PRO TIP RECAP:

#1 – BE SPECIFIC AND INTENTIONAL WHEN CRAFTING YOUR GOALS

#2 – NEVER ASK GOD TO ORDER YOUR STEPS IF YOU'RE NOT WILLING TO MOVE YOUR FEET

#3 – IF YOU WANT TO BE SUCCESSFUL, BE CONSISTENT

#4 – CREATE A GRAND VISION FOR YOUR LIFE

Based off the tips in this chapter, how will you create an intentional vision for your life?

1.)

2.)

3.)

Notes

Notes

PRINCIPLE: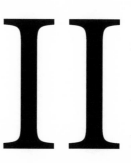

"Getting around the right people is

the biggest success hack in the world."

- Anonymous

Whether you know it or not, a lot of your current and future success solely depends on those that you have around you. Ask any billionaire, millionaire, or successful person in their own respect, and they will tell you that a major factor in their journey to the top was their team of top tier personal advisors (or crew, squad, homies, rollies, etc. for all of my Millennials and Gen Z-ers out there.)

I learned a very important lesson in choosing the people that you're around at a young age. When I was in the 6th grade, I was timid, meek, and incredibly studious. According to my classmates, I was a nerd to the 12th power. I was the kid who wore a pocket protector, always made sure my pants were tucked well over my mid-section. In other words: a *fashion tragedy*. I carried EVERY textbook with me at all times, and I was enrolled in honors classes. I was super shy, so finding friends was far and few between. Until the day I met 'The Danielle's'.

This particular group of young ladies were all named Danielle, and they just so happened to be the biggest and baddest crew that ever walked the halls of my middle school. You can imagine my surprise when they summoned me to become apart of their prestigious clique of adolescents.

You see, this marked a major turning point in my pubescent life. Being able to walk the halls of my middle school with the most popular crew in the 6th grade definitely took me to an elevated social status. I started hanging out with the girls daily after school and quickly learned that I was more of *their* friend than they were mine. I was doing their homework, lying for them as they skipped classes, and whatever other mischievous activity you can think of. Totally out of my norm.

It wasn't until a very specific incident happened that made me question their loyalty more than ever. I had recently returned to school from a trip to New York with my family, and to my surprise, I was sent to the office no sooner than I arrived through the doors.

"Suspended?!"

I shrieked as tears began to well in my eyes. I had never even received a tardy for being late so the thought of being suspended was absolutely beyond me.

"There must be a mistake?!" I pleaded with the school secretary.

"Danielle Hughes, correct?" she counter argued. I slowly shook my head in disbelief. "Yeah, no mistakes here, kid. 3-day suspension."

There I was… sitting in the school office, hysterically crying because the world (my 11-year-old world) as I knew it was crumbling around me. I sat in the school office for what seemed to be hours waiting to be picked up. The car ride home was long and grueling. Several thoughts ran through my mind… how did I let this happen? How did the president of the entire 6th grade class (yes, that was I) get suspended? My mind was racing a million miles a minute.

Prior to me leaving school for the day, the secretary slipped a manila folder into my backpack. I'm not sure what made me remember that folder, but I quickly grabbed my backpack and snatched the folder apart. Inside I found a detailed report explaining my suspension. Apparently, I was caught lingering in the hallways after the bell rang for homeroom. The only issue here is that the date on the pale pink permission slip didn't match up with my travel dates from NY.

You see, I returned to school on a Tuesday, and according to the suspension paperwork, the incident occurred the day that I was out of town. A light bulb went off in my head, and I began to put two and two together. If I wasn't at school that day, who could've given my name?

Yep, you guessed it.

The Danielle's.

I guess you can say that this was my first experience in betrayal and learning who my friends were.

When you bring new people around your mom and she says, "Those aren't your friends!" Listen to her. She is correct. (99.9% of the time, anyway.) Love ya, mom!

My pubescent brain couldn't even begin to fathom such a betrayal from my beloved group of namesakes'. *What did I do wrong? Why would they choose to give ME up?*

PRO TIP 5

Learn who is for you and who is not. Clearly, the Danielle's weren't for me. Your tribe should be able to uplift, inspire, correct, and support you. Every audience isn't yours, every client isn't yours, and every group of people isn't for YOU. Now, in life or in business, I'm sure you won't deal with any situations such as getting suspended due to a group of backstabbing 6th graders, but life happens. Watching the company you keep and knowing when and how to exit relationships is probably the number one most important key to success. Also, don't get discouraged when you find out that someone isn't who they portrayed themselves to be. It's life. If you haven't experienced this yet, you will... and guess what? You'll survive!

I'll tell you exactly what I did wrong...

I once read a quote that described the beauty of trees shedding leaves in the fall that I'll always remember:

"The trees are about to show us how lovely it is to let the dead things go." –Anonymous

This quote can apply to several factors in life, but just about everyone can attest that this metaphor directly applies to our relationships with others. As I stated earlier, *"Watching the company you keep and knowing when and how to exit relationships is probably the number one most important key to success."* I know that a great deal of anything I've accomplished in life thus far was a direct reflection of the people I had around me. Letting go of a friendship, relationship, career, or anything else that is no longer positively serving you can be one of the best decisions you can make. Fortunately, I was fired from most of the dead-end jobs that I've encountered throughout my lifetime, but if you're currently unhappy with where you are in life – whether it is with your relationships, jobs, etc, I suggest that you fire whatever it is that you feel you've outgrown or has no opportunity for growth. Yep, you read that right. FIRE THEM.

I attend several conferences and professional development workshops per year, but it was a quote that I heard at a *Forbes Under 30* Summit that is permanently engraved in my brain.

"You need to fire twice as much as you hire."

I can't remember who exactly quoted this, but I do know that it stuck with me. This quote doesn't just relate to business, but in your interpersonal relationships and friendships as well. I've found that you're only as good as those that you have around you. When you've found that you've outgrown a situation, person, etc., it's best to cut ties immediately. Hanging on to something or someone that you know is just a dead end does nothing but stagnate growth.

You want to grow or nah?!

Speaking of growth, I think it's very important to note that it is natural. If something isn't growing, then it's dead (or fake... fake plants don't grow either. Fake people might, but fake plants don't.)

In high school, I won "Social Butterfly" during our senior year mock elections. Looking back, I'm always so surprised at how different of a person I am now as opposed to then. You couldn't PAY me to stay at home on the weekends when I was younger. If I wasn't out in the mix, then I was losing my mind. I easily had 30-40 friends texting me per day about Lord knows what from sun up to sundown. I used to pride myself on that. Being invited to all of the hotspots, hanging out every weekend, and knowing everyone's business.

You know what that looks like to me now? Exhausting.

I can't even fathom giving out that much energy per day now unless it's going towards something productive. Outside of business interactions, I can count on one hand how many people I deal with on a personal level per day. Protecting my energy and preserving my peace has become a non-negotiable for me. Once I did a thorough detox of the relationships in my life, things drastically changed for the better. At one point, every time I dropped a connection that I knew was no longer serving me, I received either some amazing opportunity or more money... I kid you not! It's almost like God was rewarding me for letting them go. I have since learned to take heed and follow my intuition when I know that a person or opportunity is not for me. I make peace with the situation and gracefully move forward. I hope you will too.

I strongly suggest that you continuously detox your life. That means your diet, the contacts in your cell phone, your car, your bedroom, and most importantly your mind.

PRO TIP 6

Growth is natural. Let the dead weight go. Ladies, there is a reason why your stylist insists that you get your ends trimmed every so often. Not only does it just look raggedy (you're not trying to be out here raggedy, are you?) but, those dead ends stop your hair from growing. You see where I'm going with this? Fellas, unless you have a head full of hair, you probably can't relate to that, but I hope you'll relate to this: Let. It. Go. Whatever "it" may be for you. If you've been looking for a sign, you just found it. Go forth and manifest healthy, loving, supportive relationships that won't end in a fireball of confusion. You're going to have to let go of a lot to unlock the next level of your life. Go head... start now!

I had a crew of 5 friends back in high school. We did everything together. I mean *everything!* You didn't see one without the other. We were tight. My relationship with all of them remained pretty close up until a few years ago. I began progressing in my relationship with God, my spirituality, my purpose, and my personal brand. This is not to say that they weren't progressing as well, their growth just wasn't conducive to *mine.* The relationships between the girls and I, with the exception of two, naturally began to fall apart.

Once you're doing the work to "level up" in life, you'll naturally fall into spaces and places that better serve your energy. Now, if you're exerting nasty, polluted energy equipped with bad, self-depreciating thoughts, then that's exactly what you're going to get back. Adversely, if your focus is on bettering yourself, your environment, and the people around you, then you're bound to receive that back to you tenfold. It's nature's law.

HIS STORY: Chigozie (Chi) Uwazurike, Serial Entrepreneur, Le Don Collection, LLC.

The importance of building a power team is very essential in our discourse today because we are more likely to perform well when we work effectively as a team. I'm an entrepreneur and a tastemaker, which requires a team in order to create an impeccable synergy. The combined effect of a team is always greater than the sum of individual efforts. Businesses like Le Don Collection LLC., Rare Boutique LLC., and Young & Productive Vintage Life LLC., were all built on enhancement and performances due to great teamwork and partnership. What is a tastemaker? A tastemaker is a trendsetter or person who influences what is or will become fashionable. When curating an event, I usually need help planning. This is especially true on the day of the actual event which usually gets stressful. Without a solid team behind me, it would be very difficult to carry out each task effectively. Everybody on my team has a position, and that makes it very easy to understand what roles each person plays. Building a team can be very excruciating at times, but the best way to study and understand your team is to learn what their strengths and weaknesses are. When running a business, the first thing I'm looking for is a team that can react and move efficiently. This is the best way to identify which areas are their strengths, and also focus on their weaknesses until they become their strongest skills. There are so many benefits that pertain to having a great team within a business or company like improving flexibility, having productive meetings, sharing innovative ideas, and increasing stock. Teamwork will drastically increase efficiency and productivity. In other words, enhancement, learning, and progress are not attributed to individual efforts, but rather a joint collaboration.

Nevertheless, teamwork is a result of a coordinated group effort amongst people working together to achieve a common goal. Although I believe in teamwork and the importance of building a strong team behind me, some people aren't always predisposed to working well with a group or team. We can argue or debate about the reasons why people wouldn't feel the need to work effectively or efficiently within a group or a team, but it is obvious that individual interests often disrupt team spirit. In my opinion, and personal experiences, people's competitive spirit and ego can end up overshadowing their instincts and clouding the main reason why they signed up to be on the team to begin with. Such a disruption may result in the company or business performing poorly or failing.

Finally, the purpose of building a power team is to create a strong framework that will increase efficiency or output. When building a power team for my business, it requires having a vision and intent to invent and re-invent ideas. Always create a strong structure within the business and surround the business with genuine people who believe in the same common goal as you. They have to feel connected to the business just as much as you do. These individuals will have to represent the business in such a way that the general public will identify them as business owners rather than employees. IG: @le_don I www.ledoncollection.com

You won't have to work hard to find your tribe once you make the decision to level up in life. The right people around you will have you closer to God, thriving in your career and business, and pushing you to live your best life.

I want you to make a list of your personal board of advisors. Not sure what that means? I'll tell you: your PBA consists of 5 people (at the very least) who help contribute to your personal and professional growth. These people hold you accountable for accomplishing your goals, offer constructive criticism to assist your growth, and serve as a source of inspiration and encouragement.

Here are some examples of the power players you should have on your team:

- **MENTOR: An experienced and trusted advisor. Someone who trains or advises.**

- **SPIRITUAL ADVISOR: A spiritual advisor really has no solid definition. The best way I can describe it is someone who can assist you in finding your spiritual direction.**

- **COACH: A person who counsels and encourages clients on matters having to deal with careers or personal challenges.**

- **FINANCIAL ADVISOR: Someone who provides sound financial advice and services to clients.**

Each of these people will serve a separate purpose in your life. Sometimes, you can even find all of these qualities in one person. I've been blessed to experience each type of person in my life. I've even found all of these qualities in one or more friends. If you don't feel like you have anyone in your life who fits these descriptions, I urge you to make the decision to create your own Personal Board of Advisors.

Mentorship is essential to success. Name any successful person you know, and I guarantee they'll tell you that having a mentor was paramount to their growth. In case you're not sure what mentorship is, let's check out the official definition:

"Mentorship is a relationship in which a more experienced or more knowledgeable person helps to guide a less experienced or less knowledgeable person." – Webster's Dictionary

A mentor can be anyone. Your grandmother, your uncle, your sibling or even a peer. No matter what you make it out to be, you need a mentor.

Let me share with you why…

It was June 5th, 2015. The time was about 11:30 a.m., and I was being escorted to my car with a box of my belongings by my boss and the head of our HR department. If you can't already tell where this story is going, I'll give you a hint: I got fired. *(I told you that would be a common theme in this book.)*

Just a few weeks prior to my firing, the coworker that helped hire me was pleading with me on the phone to just "prove everyone wrong" and stick it out. Taking this new position was a huge learning curve for me and I was failing miserably.

I guess I hadn't proved everyone wrong.

I sat in my car and bawled my eyes out. I literally just packed up my life and moved 16 hours away from home, and here I was… in the parking lot of a TV news station in the middle of nowhere with barely any money and to add to that… no job.

Let me backtrack a bit…

As I previously mentioned, it had been my dream since I was 16 years old to become a News Anchor. It wasn't until my 11th grade English teacher assigned a 'where do you see yourself in 10 years' essay that I decided to act on it.

See, I had never put much thought into where I wanted to be when I grew up. I just knew I wanted to be poppin'.

Ms. Johnson instructed my class of high school juniors to stand in a circle and share the vision that we each had for the next 10 years of our lives. My peers shared their dreams of becoming entrepreneurs, doctors, community activists, etc., and when it became my turn to speak, I did what I knew best… made a scene.

"Well, Danielle! Your turn. Where do you see yourself in 10 years?" Ms. Johnson nudged.

"I don't know. I want to be famous." I shrugged.

"Danielle! You write a paper about being 'famous' and I'm FAILING you!" She barked.

I rolled my eyes and proceeded to mutter under my breath: "I'm still writing the paper."

To make a long story short, I didn't end up writing a paper about being famous, but I *did* end up at WDIV Detroit, one of the highest rated TV news stations in the Midwest. Thanks to my uncle who had been working as a radio personality for years, I had the chance to job shadow one of their top African-American female anchors.

It was at that very moment that I fell in love with the television business… or at least I thought.

Despite it only being one day of job shadowing, I immediately became infatuated with the bright lights, the fast pace of the newsroom, and the adrenaline of breaking news.

I went on to move to Atlanta to pursue my undergraduate degree in Journalism. While there, I became president of the student chapter of the National Association of Black Journalists. While at a meeting for the city chapter, we were suddenly rearranged into groups as a burly voice called out, "IT'S MENTOR MATCH DAY!"

Hol' up… I didn't sign up for all of this.

I turned to my left and to my right to see what the heck was going on. All around me, people were scurrying to find a match. Because I had no clue what was going on, I just stood in the middle of the room and waited for someone to find me.

"Well, I guess that makes us a match? We're the only two left." I heard someone chuckle while tapping my shoulder.

That person ended up becoming my mentor and the

woman that guided me through the next couple of years of my TV news career. It was short lived but, hey, it happened.

Fast forward to 2015…

After being let go from my position as a reporter in Alabama, I had no clue what would be next for me. As I sat in my car, sobbing uncontrollably, a light bulb began to go off.

'Call your mentor.'

I hopped on the highway and proceeded to dial her number. It's almost like she knew that something was wrong because she immediately answered.

"What's wrong?"

I guess she knew that something was up because I was calling her at 10 am. I proceeded to tell her what just happened. She took a deep breath and told me to hop on the road to Atlanta to the station where she worked because she had a plan.

I dried my tears, went to my apartment, and packed up my tiny, compact car to hit the road to Atlanta. It took me almost 3 hours to get there from rural Alabama, but I made it. I pulled up to the station literally minutes before she was to anchor the 6pm newscast. As I hurried into the studio to watch her before she went live, she gave me the thumbs up and whispered; "It's handled."

Once the newscast ended, she and I congregated at the anchor desk as she went on to tell me that she made a phone call to her old news director in a city about 2 ½ hours outside of Atlanta and that the woman wanted to interview me for a reporter position.

We fist bumped and she told me that the woman would be calling me later on that week.

As promised, she called me. Her name was Elaine. She explained that she was the news director at a local station in Georgia, and she wanted to hire me as a reporter at the station.

"Hire me?!" I thought. She didn't even interview me. Why would she want to hire me?

Elaine went on to say that my mentor spoke so highly of me and my work ethic that she didn't feel the need to interview me. In fact, she wanted to offer me a position as the morning show anchor making $15,000 more than I was making at the station I was just fired from. Not too bad for a 23-year-old fresh out of college.

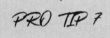

PRO TIP 7

Mentors are IMPERATIVE. If we've ever had a conversation or you've ever browsed any of my social media, I'm sure I drilled the importance of mentorship. I truly believe that every single person on this earth needs a mentor... or two... or three, etc. It was all in God's plan for me to get fired and be introduced to Elaine. My mentor was the bridge that connected it all. Now, I can't guarantee that your stuation will turn out exactly like mine did, but I can guarantee that having a mentor is like having a personal navigation system that helps to guide you along the right path. Whether that's personal, business, or everything else in between. Find someone who will nurture and encourage you, but most importantly - correct you. Don't know how to find a mentor? Make a list of ten things you're looking for in one. Now, take the top 5 from that list and actively search to find someone. Keep in mind, this person does not have to look like you, have the same background as you, or even the same profession. As long as you believe this person can hold you accountable to you being your best self and provide you with sound advice, go for it! I have several mentors now, and I have nothing physically in common with most of them. What we do have in common is our willingness to be better each day, and I believe that's what it's all about.

My very first mentor in TV, Mark Winne, taught me the importance of social media/branding etiquette very early on. When we met, I was a 21-year-old intern at the station where he was working. He asked to see all of the interns' social media accounts so he could give us feedback since we were all burgeoning young professionals. Make a long story short, my screen name across all of my social media profiles was @daniondemand. He assured me that I sounded like an adult film star and that I should probably start using the name I was born with. Thus, Danielle D. Hughes was born! Mark taught me much more than how to refine my image on the internet, including how to negotiate my first big TV contract, the importance of being authentic and transparent in your work, and how to keep a good name in business. All were very important tips that I keep near and dear to this day. He also allowed me to spend every Thanksgiving that I was away from home with him and his family. Good mentors always inevitably turn into family members. (That is, if they feel as if the relationship is mutually beneficial.)

Now that we've discussed mentors... let's talk about the importance of being a good mentee.

As much as we want our mentors to pour into us, it's equally important (if not more) that we pour into them as well. I suggest that you seek someone that is consistent and willing to take the necessary time to properly mentor you. As a mentee, you should also be consistent.

In 2015, a young lady reached out to me via Instagram asking if I would mentor her. She explained that she was a college student studying broadcast journalism and wondered if I would be willing to be her mentor.

I am very intentional with choosing mentees these days, just because I have had my time wasted by so many people in the past. Bria was different, though. From the beginning, she understood that this was a two-way

Hi Danielle!

My name is Bria Brown. I'm a senior at Oakland University (graduating December 19) studying journalism and I'm an aspiring news anchor. I've been following your page for a long time & it is very encouraging & inspiring! I believe you're from Detroit, right? I would love to talk to you one day & maybe get some advice from you about being in this industry?

Looking forward to hearing from you!

street and that she was going to get out of it what she put in.

Not only is she consistent, (which is very important to me) she is a motivated self-starter who creates her own opportunities. Bria is also patient and does not send several texts or emails when I'm taking a while to get back with her. More than likely, your mentor or potential mentor is juggling several things at once. Following up a few times is great, but after that I would highly suggest waiting for their response or reaching out to someone else whom you believe will best fit your needs.

There is a fine line between being persistent and being a bug-a-boo. Don't be a bug-a-boo.

Because of Bria's persistence, she has been able to create her own opportunities. I made it my mission to open her eyes to all of the things I wish I would've known at her age in hopes that she wouldn't have to learn lessons the hard way as I did. From branding herself professionally, to sound financial habits, and strengthening both of our relationships with God - I can truly say that we have a mutually beneficial relationship. As much as she says that she has grown, I believe that I have as well.

Bria recently accepted a major position in her career field, and I felt as if I just accepted a new job offer as well. I honestly feel like her win is my win.

QUICK NOTE ON PAYING IT FORWARD: I guarantee that someone has helped you get to where you currently are in life. A few ways that you can give back include, taking a mentee under your wing, paying for a personal development course, providing scholarships or just being a listening ear. However you decide to pay it forward, make sure that you're pulling others as

you climb. Someone has invested in you and your success. It's only right that you do the same for others.

One of my sister-friends, Meagan Ward, created a course entitled "Manifesting Mentorship." The 6-week course introduced people seeking mentors to the basics of mentorship. Her mission was to equip millennials in the city of Detroit with the tools to attract and maintain high quality mentor/mentee relationships.

I asked her to share some of her biggest tips for those seeking mentors:

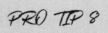

PRO TIP 8

MENTEE TIPS & ETIQUETTE AS TOLD BY MEAGAN WARD:

1) Be clear on your WHY. Why do you want a mentor? What exactly do you want out of the relationship? Getting clear on this will make the process of selecting a mentor much easier!

2) Figure out who exactly you're looking for. How can this person get you to the next level? What type of qualities are you seeking? Can they support you mentally, emotionally, and physically in the pursuit of your dreams?

3) Come CORRECT. Make sure that you're presenting yourself as professional as possible. First impressions last!

4) Be respectful of your mentor's time. Keep in mind that they're likely very busy. Do your homework/research before each meeting, and always come prepared.

5) Set attainable and realistic goals. You are not your mentor's only responsibility. Please do not mistake them for a life coach and expect for them to solve all of your problems. They are busy professionals, as are you!

6) Be a mentee that your mentors are excited to advocate for. A mentor/mentee relationship should be MUTUALLY beneficial.

Thanks for that, Meagan! Which leads me to my next point...

The people you choose to surround yourself with are imperative to your growth and success. I have been very intentional over the past couple of years of weeding out who no longer seemed to fit or forced me to "level up." My 'sister-friends' as I affectionately call them consist of 5 of my closest girlfriends. Remember what I said earlier in this chapter about your power players? Well, I've been blessed to find those qualities in each of the women that I have in my circle. (FYI: I have several male friends who pour into me just as much as my girls do, but this chapter isn't about them.)

Let's take Erin for instance. Erin White, or Dr. White (I

just call her "Sista") is one of my oldest friends and confidants. Our friendship is a true example of friends that force you to get it together and step your game up.

I recently started therapy, and I can honestly say that Erin was the main person pushing me to do so. She is currently enrolled in a doctorate program in Psychology... the reason why I called her Dr. White! Erin holds me accountable, corrects me, but most of all loves and prays for me. I couldn't ask for more in a friend. You'll hear more from her later.

Leveling up comes in many different forms, and this just so happens to be how I define it.

PRO TIP 9

Getting around the right people is the biggest success hack in the world. You are who you spend the most time with. If you're unhappy with where you are in life, one of the most important things to do is take an assessment of those you have around you. If you're the smartest person in your circle, then it's time for a new circle. Get a squad that forces you to level up spiritually, financially, physically, and emotionally. Sit with the winners... the conversation is different.

PRO TIP RECAP:

#5 – LEARN WHO IS FOR YOU AND WHO IS NOT

#6 – GROWTH IS NATURAL. LET THE DEAD WEIGHT GO

#7 – MENTORS ARE IMPERATIVE

#8 – MENTEE TIPS/ETIQUETTE

#9 – GETTING AROUND THE RIGHT PEOPLE IS THE BIGGEST SUCCESS HACK IN THE WORLD

Based off the tips in this chapter, in what ways can you create new relationships in your life (or strengthen the ones that you already have) that your future self will thank you for?

1.)

2.)

3.)

Notes

PRINCIPLE:

The Chapter About Money

(...and credit + saving + budgeting)

"Save your money, kids.

Life comes at you fast."

–Charlamagne Tha God

"DANI!!!"

My sister frantically screamed while bolting down the basement steps. I was sleeping on the pull-out bed in my parents' basement when my sister aggressively shook me out of my slumber. It was 5:00 in the morning, and the sky was a beautiful shade of fuchsia.

"There are some men outside taking your car! Hurry! Get up! NOW."

I shot up from the flimsy mattress and quickly flew up the flight of stairs. As I made my way to the front door, I was greeted by a piercing bright light being shined in my eyes. As I fought to see what was on the other side, I heard a terribly raspy voice sarcastically smirk in a New York accent,

"Say goodbye to ya car, Sweetheart! It's going bye-bye!"

At that very moment, I watched my brand new, shiny, midnight black SUV being wheeled out of my parents' driveway by a tow truck. I still reminisce on the disappointment in my stepdad's face to this day. He slowly shook his head and whispered,

"Why didn't you say anything?"

I thought I had let my parents down so much in the last year that I didn't know how I could possibly come back from this. My chest felt like I had been hit with a baseball bat. The tears began to swell, and I dropped to my knees as I slowly began to weep.

My car was being repossessed.

I looked to the sky and thought, *"What did I do to deserve this?!"*

I'll tell you what I did: I didn't pay my car note. For months.

I ended up borrowing the money from my parents to retrieve the car from the repo lot. I was making roughly $280 per week while substitute teaching and had fallen behind on bills. I was too embarrassed to speak up and admit that I hadn't actually paid a car note in 3 months. This was the second time in my life that I realized I had to do better with my money, and I vowed to never allow myself to get to that point again.

***

When I was younger, my grandmother (I just call her Granny) would sit at her kitchen table and make the most meticulous budgets I've ever seen. I would watch in awe as she would take she and my grandfather's cash for the week and strategically place them in specific envelopes.

Although I've had my fair share of financial mistakes, all of those years of watching my granny handle her money definitely rubbed off on me. Now keep in mind that I am no financial advisor. I've just learned how to save some coins.

I first realized that I had a knack (or obsession) with money when I was in the 3rd grade, and my elementary school was having its annual book fair. As I stared out into a sea of 8-year-olds making a mad dash for the latest *Captain Underpants* series, my eyes were suddenly fixed on a book from the American Girl series called *MONEYMAKERS: Good Cents for Girls*. I found the book a couple of months ago while cleaning out my room at my mom's house. I'd say it was love at first sight… or love at first read. Besides my grandmother, that book would serve as my first real introduction to financial literacy. It is also one of the major reasons that you're reading this book today.

Most of the young people I've worked with have no clue about their credit score, budgeting, or investing. I created a goal setting + financial planning workbook entitled *My Million Dollar Workbook* with the intention of educating young people on the importance of understanding their finances just for that reason.

My 20's have served as a pretty exhilarating, eye-opening, beautifully strange time in my life for my finances. To make things even more complicated, while trying to figure myself out I've had to take adulting to the next level and figure out my money too. For the majority of our lives all money matters were handled for us, and sometimes that's not a good thing.

Believe it or not, generational curses can be passed down through many different avenues: one of them being our finances.

As a child, your first role models (most likely) are your parents. Their ways are your ways, and their thoughts are your thoughts. Parents and legal guardians carry the responsibility of teaching us how to do many things, but how to *properly* manage finances doesn't always make the cut. I can't recall a time where saving, budgeting, investing, or the importance of great credit was ever talked about in my household. Not because my parents didn't want to talk about it, but because they simply did not *know.*

If simple conversations about saving and budgeting were

never talked about in my household, I could only *imagine* that others my age were never taught these basic fundamentals as well.

In the words of one of my favorite financial advisors, Pete The Planner:

"Controlling your cash flow is the single most financially responsible thing you can do."

Let me say, I've been in situations where I've had a lot of money and situations where I've had none (like having $5 in my account... yeah, that broke.)

It is true that money doesn't buy happiness, but it does provide stability.

First things first...

Deposit Accounts

SAVINGS	$5.00
XXXXXX6800-S01	Avail: $0.00
CHOICE CHECKING	($97.34)
XXXXXX6800-S02	Avail: ($97.34)
CENTSIBLE SAVINGS	$2.43
XXXXXX6800-S03	Avail: $2.43
Total:	($89.91)

Loan Accounts

Total:	$0.00

SAVING: If you do not have at least $1,000 saved that you can access right now, I suggest that you start there. It is ideal to have 3-24 months' worth of income saved for emergencies. Having a bit of a cushion will allow you to have a sense of peace when life happens (... and it WILL happen!)

If you're looking to build your savings, I like to stick to the 50/20/30 rule.

- **50% = ESSENTIAL MONTHLY EXPENSES:** Gas for work, phone and internet, rent/mortgage, groceries, utilities, car insurance and/or car payment, credit card/minimum loan payment.

- **30% = LIFESTYLE:** Dining out, vacations, entertainment, shopping, etc.

- **20% = FINANCIAL PRIORITIES:** Savings, investments, and debt repayment.

The *ideal* budget would look a little like this:

- **HOUSING: 25%**

- **TRANSPORTATION: 15%**

- **GROCERIES AND DINING OUT: 12%**

- **SAVINGS: 10%**

- **UTILITIES AND PHONE: 10%**

- **CHARITY: 5%**

- **CLOTHING: 5%**

- **ENTERTAINMENT: 5%**

- **MEDICAL: 5%**

- **MISCELLANEOUS: 3%**

Notice, I said ideal. If this doesn't work for you – that's fine! This is a pretty good starting point if you're having trouble making and sticking to a budget though.

No matter which way you spin it, saving is something

that takes some getting used to. However, over time I've found the secret to effective spending, and that is creating a budget and sticking to it! The easiest way to begin your budget is to make a list of all of the things you typically spend money on each month. Make sure that you're being as specific as possible. The earlier you begin to become realistic about spending triggers, the easier it is to manage them. Going through online bank statements helps with this tremendously!

Creating a budget will allow you to be transparent with yourself and see where you're spending more or less in certain areas. Once you've created a healthy budget, you'll want to find ways to make your budget leaner by cutting back on expenses. It also helps to be realistic about needs vs. wants.

Food = A need.

Spending hundreds of dollars a month on 5-star restaurants = A want.

List your needs vs. wants and figure out what you absolutely cannot live without. For me, I love new cars and music. That's my vice. As a result, I am currently leasing my vehicle and paying a car note, and I pay $9.99 for Apple Music each month faithfully. I'm not saying this will work for you, but it works for my budget. I got serious about my 'non-negotiables' (what I'm not willing to compromise on each month) and those two just so happened to make my list. I am able to cut back in a lot of other areas, however. I would consider myself extremely frugal, so I try my best to save at least 30% of my take home pay and only splurge on things that I absolutely need. For example, when making my first "real" budget, I decided that I was spending a ridiculous amount on getting my nails done. So, I stopped.

I stopped paying to get my nails done 7 years ago. I've only had them painted maybe 3 times since then for special occasions. Prior to that, I was at the nail salon FAITHFULLY every two weeks! Since becoming clear on what was important to me and my money, I've replaced my nail money with "play money" meaning that I use it for dining out, entertainment, or whatever else my heart desires. I'm not saying that this will work for you – we're all different – but I guarantee that taking a full assessment of what you're spending per month will open your eyes to several different ways that you can cut back and save. Take just an hour to sit down and get a clear view of your finances, and I guarantee you'll be surprised on how much you've been spending on frivolous expenses.

I do a few things each month that allow me to stick to my financial goals:

- Review my budget often. (I definitely check it weekly but checking monthly will suffice as well.)

- Keep my wallet neat and orderly.

- Set up a schedule to pay my bills.

- Keep up with receipts. (I keep every receipt. You never know how they'll come in handy!)

I've included '6 Easy Money Saving Tips' to make this process a bit easier! These tips can also be found in my *Million Dollar Workbook* at danielledhughes.com.

1. COOK INSTEAD OF EATING OUT

Going out to eat might be more convenient, but it's only hurting your pockets in the long run. Try organizing your week by figuring out when you'll have time to plan a meal and actually stick to it. Weekly meal prepping saves you tons of time *and* money.

2. USE CASH

Using debit and credit cards while making purchases is all fun and games until you're going back through your bank statements and realize how much money you've frivolously spent because you couldn't *see* it. You're less likely to spend while using cash because your subconscious is more aware of losing the money when you can see and feel it.

3. BUY USED

There is absolutely nothing wrong with buying used especially if you're saving yourself hundreds (or even thousands) of dollars. Online platforms such as Craigslist will aid you in finding quality clothing, furniture, cars, and electronics while still ballin' on a budget.

4. UNPLUG ELECTRONICS WHEN NOT IN USE

This tip will not only help save money on your electric bill but preserve battery life to your electronics. Certain electronics take up a lot of energy. While you're away from home, make it a habit to unplug the nonessentials in your home especially during winter. Video game consoles, cell phones, televisions, etc. The money that you can save while doing this over the course of a year is mind blowing!

5. SHOP AROUND

Before making a big purchase, wait a day or two to see if you can find the same product or a similar version for any cheaper. Flex your financial discipline muscles, and shop around to compare prices.

6. FREE & CHEAP OUTINGS

There is a section in one of the local papers that I frequently read titled "Free and Cheap." The purpose? To showcase free and cheap events surrounding the area that I live in. There are tons of ways to enjoy yourself with less than $10. Get creative and hop on Pinterest, (to design an ideal day for cheap) or inquire about what moderately priced events are happening in your area. Your pockets will thank you.

There have been a couple times in my life where I've been at my lowest point financially. One was the time I got my car repossessed. The second was college.

I went off to college with $800 in my savings account from the money I'd saved from my job at a youth center in metro Detroit. That was my first 'big girl' job and the only one I've never been fired from. I'd like to think that's because it was so closely related to my purpose. More on that later.

I worked several jobs in undergrad while taking a full course load of classes. My $800 quickly dwindled once I became accustomed to life on campus, and I knew that moving back to Detroit was not an option. I had two options: sink or swim.

I decided to swim.

I remember calling my mom crying hysterically because I was working two jobs (one overnight), interning, and enrolled in school full time. I thought it was just "too much." I didn't have a car or a license, so I had to walk and take the train or bus. I was walking at least a mile or two to get where I needed to be each day. I was tired and losing hope. I'm all for working smarter, but I truly believe that sometimes you have to put your feet to the pavement and get moving. You cannot cheat the grind. You get in what you put out.

I knew that if I did not work to support myself, I would not have the money to continue living in Atlanta. I tried my hardest not to call home for anything until I literally came to the point where I cleared out my savings account in an attempt to pay for expenses associated with my summer courses. I had recently loaned my boyfriend at the time $1500 (which was 85% of my savings) because he was mismanaging his money. He assured me over and over again that I would receive the money back, and to this day I haven't seen a dime of it. That situation took me into a downward spiral because I allowed my pride to take over, and I suffered in silence for many months following that incident. Instead of calling home and asking to borrow money, I suffered… for a long time. There were days when I would have to depend on free events on campus just to eat because I had only $3 or less in my accounts. The McDonald's near Grady Hospital would become my go-to because I knew that I could eat for $5 or less and be satisfied. Most days, that was the only meal that I would have in an entire day.

I began sneaking my roommate's groceries without her consent because I was too prideful to ask for anything. She began to notice that the food in her cabinet was dwindling and decided to confront me about it one day. My first reaction was to lie, but instead I ended up breaking down and explaining my situation to her. To my surprise, she was extremely understanding and assured me that it was okay to ask for help because we all need it sometimes. To this day, I still think about her helpfulness and grace during that time. People like that don't come around often!

I decided that I was tired of living the way I was. I was tired of putting on a front and having to mask my true living situation. So, I sucked up my pride and called home... I reached out to my Nana (my Grandmother on my Dad's side) to be exact.

After explaining to my Nana what was happening, she lovingly scolded me and said that what I was experiencing was all a part of the process. She explained that I was having growing pains and it happens to everyone (in some form or another) while trying to chase a dream. She asked that I send her my bank information and said that she would transfer some money over. My Nana probably doesn't even realize this, but that initial investment into my account set the tone for how I would handle my money from there on out.

Two days later, I had $400 in my bank account.

$400!

At this point, I thought I was rich. From that moment, I knew that I would never allow myself to be in that position again. I just couldn't do it. I began to become very intentional about the time that I spent with my money. I put myself on a very strict budget and started to invest time in learning how to make my money work for me. Rich Dad, Poor Dad became my favorite book, and I began moving a lot differently as it related to my finances.

I built my account back up and decided it was time to learn more about my credit score. I had no clue what my score was or how to go about retrieving it. I hopped online and found a couple of free resources to help me get a ball park range of my credit score. To my surprise, it was in the high 600's. I did a little more research and decided to open my first credit card which leads me to my next point.

If you're not familiar with your credit score, you should be! Credit is borrowed money that allows you to purchase things and the likelihood that you will pay back those loans to purchase more things.

Loren Entsuah, CEO of Entsuah Financial Group, LLC.

A majority of us want money, or would like to increase our income, however many of us do not understand how money truly works. Money is a tool that is used to obtain things you want and need. This message coincides with the top percentile of the wealth in the world, and they approach money accordingly. Everyday we make purchases and use cash to do so, however 72% of the world isn't creating leverage while doing this. Us as the minority are the furthest behind when it comes to this aspect of being a consumer.

If you have a semi decent credit score (600-640), it would be wise to obtain a store card at your favorite local stores, and use their point and reward system to earn free items, discounts, and improve your credit score at the same time. For example, if you shop at Target, it would be wise to get their credit card. You save 5% on every purchase made with them, and you build your credit at the same time. The same principles apply with Nordstrom. With purchases you build Nordstrom Points which eventually equate to "Notes" which are gift certificates. These notes can then be used by the account holder to save money on future purchases.

Once you have mastered this skill, you will have an abundance of credit cards which will improve your overall revolving credit limit. I always advise people to treat all of their credit cards like an AMEX Centurion, which has no credit limit, but requires all purchases that are made within the billing cycle to be paid off in full at the end. Moving forward, when you make a purchase, (and especially a larger purchase 1k or better,) know that it is a good rule of thumb to not even complete the purchase until you have half of the amount you about to spend in cash to apply as a payment the following day. Then pay the remaining balance within the 30 days that are left on that specific billing cycle.

By doing this, it allows you to beat the credit card companies at their own game. They hope that you carry a balance on your credit cards so that the issuing card bank can charge you interest monthly and make money from your ignorance. This helps you avoid paying interest, build your credit history as well as improve your chances of being awarded a credit limit increase.

7 months of this continuously will lead to a FICO Score over

700. Trust me; I am living proof!

@entsuahfinancialgroup I www.theefg.com

In other words, your credit score is your *adult* report card. Credit scores range from 300-850.

- Excellent = 750+

- Good = 700-749

- Fair = 650-699

- Poor = 600-649

- Bad = Below 599

Five different factors make up you credit score:

1. **Payment History:** *Are you paying your bills on time?*

2. **Length of Credit History:** *How long have you had credit?*

3. **Debt-to-Credit Ratio:** *Add up your total reoccurring bills and divide by your gross monthly income and voila!*

4. **New Credit Inquiries:** *Have you opened any accounts recently? or Applied for credit from anywhere?*

5. **Diversity of Credit:** *How diverse is your credit? Do you have a mix of credit, good debt, etc?*

If you do not know your credit score, you can pull your FREE (yes, free!) credit report from mycreditreport.com. Some free credit check sites that I frequent are Credit Karma, Credit.

com, and my personal favorite: creditscorecard.com.

In the words of one of my favorite authors Paulo Coehlo, "When you want something, all the universe conspires in helping you achieve it."

My challenge to all of you is to use the budget tracker and savings chart below. If you're looking to receive lifetime copies to reuse, please visit danielledhughes.com and download your copy of **'My Million Dollar Workbook.'**

BUDGET *Tracker*

	BUDGET AMT	ACTUAL AMT	DIFFERENCE	NOTES
INCOME				
Income Total				
Other Income				
EXPENSES				
Mortgage/Rent				
Household Maintenance				
Taxes				
Insurance				
Electricity				
Water				
Sewage				
Gas				
Phone				
Trash				
Cable				
Cell Phone				
Groceries				
Entertainment				
Charity/Donations				
Fuel				
Auto Insurance				
Car Payment				
Child Care				
Creadit Cards/Debt				
Loans				
Life Insurance				
Health Insureace				
Clothing				
Childsuport/Aimony				
Other				
SAVINGS				
Retirement				
College				
Basic/other				
TOTAL				

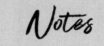

Notes

Notes

PRINCIPLE:

The Bounce Back

IV

"Success is how high you bounce after you hit rock bottom."

–General George Patton

"FIRED?!?! Again?!" I screamed into the phone while staring at my tear-filled face in my rearview mirror.

Pause. We'll get to the rest of that story later.

I read a quote about a couple of months ago that read "congrats on your failure!" I'm sure you're wondering how that even makes sense. Or, maybe you're just like me and you've experienced enough failure to know that you truly won't achieve true success without going through several failures.

I absolutely love talking about my failures. It's almost become one of my favorite pastimes, as it has become very therapeutic for me. Talking about failure is healthy. I believe it keeps you grounded and humble when you're reminded of what God brought you through. I know for a fact I wouldn't have made it through any of the situations that I'm about to share with you without Him!

It all started in the 2nd grade. I was attending McIntyre Elementary, and my teacher, Mrs. Francis, was evaluating my overall performance in her classroom with my Mom.

"She needs to be held back in the 2nd grade for another year." she barked.

Now, I'm not sure how exactly you fail the 2nd grade, but I was surely about to find out. Mrs. Francis went on to say that she believed that I wasn't competent enough to pass her class and proceeded to tell my parents how it was best that I stay behind to repeat the entire grade over.

My parents ended up deciding against the decision, and I progressed on to the 3rd grade (thank God) I don't believe that there is anything wrong with making the decision to hold your child back; I just don't believe that was the most proactive way to deal with my situation. Mrs. Francis supported her reasoning by saying that I daydreamed entirely too much, and it was hard to keep me on task. Well, I believe that both of those traits were integral in leading me to where I am.

PRO TIP 10

Trust your instincts and make your own decisions. You know what's best for you. I didn't necessarily make this decision, but I'm grateful my parents did for me. The same reason that someone thinks that you may fail could be the exact same reason you succeed. Trust your instincts and don't second guess yourself. You are already equipped with everything you need to succeed. Trust that and keep it moving. Nothing more. Nothing less.

Growing up, I was constantly chastised for not following rules. I believe that specific trait has aided me in becoming the leader that I am today. Ultimately, leadership is whatever you define it to be. Mine just so happens to be disruptive leadership. I'm passionate about disrupting the way that young people learn because I believe that I am a prime example of a child whose learning style was not supported by my school system. Speaking of that, my first experience with challenging the status quo happened when I was 7. I attended a private school at the time, and every so often we would go to synagogue. I'm guessing I grew tired of the curriculum because I took it upon myself to teach my entire class a verse of JT Money's song "*Who Dat*" while we were supposed to be engaged with our instructor. Needless to say, that was my last day there.

I've been about this disruptor life for a while now.

A few chapters ago, I explained that "firing" would be a common theme in this book. I've been fired a lot. 5 different times to be exact: Dairy Queen, a summer camp back in my hometown, a law office, and two TV news stations. *A lot.*

I wasn't passionate about any of those places. I tried my hardest and did my best, but I'm grateful that I was forced out of each and every one of those positions. If I wasn't, I can guarantee you that I would probably still be at a few of those places today. Miserable and unfulfilled. Thank God for forcing us out of spaces that we're not meant to be in.

PRO TIP 11

Be grateful for the re-route. I have an entire chapter dedicated to gratitude in this book. Gratitude is one of the leading factors in success. Don't believe me? Look up any of your favorite entrepreneurs', pioneers', or change-makers' thoughts on gratitude, and I guarantee that you will find that it is one of the most pivotal points of their success. I've found that God will re-route you when he sees that your plans will potentially ruin you. I've been re-routed SEVERAL times in life. I used to question why it was happening to me or why I couldn't catch a break, but I now know that nothing in life is happening to you, rather for you. Embrace the road blocks that God puts in your life, and maneuver through it. If you needed a reminder, here it is: Everything is working out for your good. Everything.

A QUICK NOTE ON MOVING AT YOUR OWN PACE: I didn't learn how to drive or receive my drivers license until I was 23. I actually had a car before I could legally drive it. A friend of mine that I grew up with at my childhood church was killed in a car accident when I was 15, and as a result of that, I vowed to never get behind the wheel of a car. Of course, I had to end up getting around and I moved to rural Alabama where there was no public transportation. So, I had to eventually get over my fear of driving, and I'm so glad I did. I wasn't ready to begin driving at 16 like the rest of my peers, so I moved at my own pace. Thank God my parents nor anyone else tried to rush me because my time to learn was predestined for me. Please keep in mind that your timing is YOUR timing. Wherever you currently are in life is exactly where you need to be. "Comparison is the thief of joy." Keep that in mind the next time your mind drifts to comparison. Your life is your life, and it is perfectly tailored to you. If you're not happy with something in your life, you have the power to change it. The worst thing you can do is compare your genius, your talents, your charisma, and charm to someone else. Move at your own pace, and don't let anyone's opinions or critiques on what they think you should be doing rush you. her story Lance

HIS STORY: Lance Woods, Co-Founder, WeRun313

It was July of 2014 in South Beach, Miami, FL. My friends and I convened for an epic 4-day vacation celebrating my 25th birthday. It had been a few years since we all connected, so we were long overdue for a fella's trip. I was preparing for this like no other, buying all types of new clothes, shoes, etc. I wanted to go on this vacation with all new everything for my first time in Miami. I remember utilizing money in my savings account to buy the things I wanted, just because I "had to do it right". We experienced night clubs, a yacht party, the beach, jet skis, and more. We did it all. I was totally living the life of a young 25-year-old, so YOLO, right? We created a very memorable experience, and it was much needed time spent with my friends, who I call my brothers. The vacation concluded, and it was time to head back to reality. A couple weeks went by, and I was back to the regularly scheduled program. I was working in Nashville, TN as a Supply Chain Analyst for a fortune 300 organization. I was a new employee at the time, having had only been on the job for a little over two months. I remember being called into the office and being told that I was terminated. This was the first time I had ever been fired from a job, so I was in total shock. It was the middle of the work day, and there I was being instructed to pack up my things and leave as soon as possible. I felt ridiculed, embarrassed, and nervous all at the same time. I'd recently resigned from a job to take this job, and now I was being fired within 90-days of working there. In addition, I just returned from that lavish vacation, so I was not in the best position financially. The timing was wrong, but simultaneously so right. I had been preparing for the past year and a half to stop working jobs to make money, in hopes of transitioning to doing work that I had a passion for. I wanted to fulfill my purpose, so I took the termination as a sign to go after what my heart truly desired, rather than chase a check. For a long time, I wanted to get connected to youth development work, but I didn't know how I would make money seeing that I didn't have much experience. What I learned was that if you focus on your craft and get connected to your purpose, the money will come, and you will never "work" a day in your life.

It was a Friday, and since I was newly unemployed, I left work, went to my apartment and decided it was time for me to return to my hometown of Detroit. I packed up a few things and drove to Detroit for the weekend. I needed to clear my head and be around family. I shared with my best friend what happened, and he invited me to speak at a Black Male Empowerment Summit the following weekend. I didn't have a job, so I stayed in Detroit at my brother's house for a week. My best friend was already doing some amazing work in the community, so he set it up to where I could be one of the presenters. I was really nervous to speak, but I wanted to tell my truth and share some valuable lessons with young people. This was an opportunity of a lifetime. I proceeded without allowing fear to get the best of me. I shared my story about my upbringing and spoke about what I was currently experiencing to an audience of over 300 young men. From there, I was able to make connections and get my feet wet with community work in Detroit. After the summit, I returned to Nashville to break my apartment lease. I sold most of my items, packed up my car the best I could, and decided to permanently return to Detroit.

When I made it back to Detroit, I hit the ground running with volunteer work. Every opportunity I had to enter schools to speak or provide mentoring for young people, I took. Money was nearly gone, but I was receiving unemployment and living with my dad and step-mom so I could keep the little bills that I had paid while I volunteered. I had faith that something was going to come of it. I was doing a lot of brainstorming one day, and I happened to stumble upon "The Future Project" during a Google search. I don't know what I typed in or what led me there, but when I went to the site, I noticed it said that Detroit was an upcoming expansion city of the organization. Since my best friend was doing phenomenal work in the community, I asked him if he'd heard of the organization.

He said "man, I thought you'd be perfect to do something like that".

He put me in contact with a local Dream Director. Later, the CEO came to visit Detroit because they were looking to hire eight new Dream Directors. I applied for the job, but due to my lack of experience I ended up not getting it. Even still, I didn't allow that to deter me from chasing what I would call a dream job. When the eight new Dream Directors were hired, I asked if I could shadow to see what they did on a daily basis. I used that time to get in front of students, speak, mentor, and present. I also supported with any events The Future Project hosted. At this point, money was almost nonexistent for me, and my dad was starting to complain about it. So, I applied for another Supply Chain position and ended up getting a job as a logistics coordinator. I did this temporarily because I needed money, but my sights were pretty much set on becoming a Dream Director. Once the opportunity came again, literally one year later, I applied and got the job. I now have been working with "The Future Project" for close to four years, and I love what I do. I love seeing young people develop and flourish from the work I am able to do with them. Every day I have an opportunity to work with young students to inspire them to become believers in their own futures, and to courageously act on it. Failure and persistence are keys to success. Each time you fail or make a bad decision, there is a teachable moment present. You then have to make a decision on whether you're going to make the same mistake or make adjustments so that you can grow from it. Even when you think life is telling you no, being persistent can knock down doors that you once thought was closed.

IG: @__LWoods I www.werun313.com

You'd think after being let go from so many different jobs that I would become numb to it. Right?!

Wrong.

Perhaps, the most emotional and intense firing I've ever experienced was from the 2nd news station that I was let go from. Maybe because I didn't think that it would happen to me again, or maybe I just couldn't fathom that I was a little over 100k in debt for a Journalism degree that I couldn't keep a job with. (FYI, I'm sure I'm paying ALL of Sallie Mae's bills with the amount I pay back for my loans each month *sigh*.)

If you recall from the last chapter, my mentor helped me secure this newest position. I was 23. A news anchor making $15,000 more than what I was previously making as an MMJ (Multimedia Journalist.) The woman who hired me, my newest boss, intimidated the crap out of me.

She was 5'2" and wore shoulder pads in her blazers. Yikes.

Elaine made it very clear – *very quickly* – that she was not going to hold my hand or coddle me in this new position. Sometimes I liked her… most times I didn't, but I always respected her. Elaine was the epitome of tough love, and although she didn't always say the things that I liked, it was exactly what I needed to hear. My skin a got a little bit thicker with each conversation that we had.

I never formally interviewed for the position, so I made the 5-hour drive from Alabama to Georgia overnight to visit my new home. The moment I arrived, Elaine scurried me into her office and sat me down.

"I see something in you," she declared, "You have a lot of work to do. You need some polishing, but I see greatness in you. You're a diamond in the rough."

I never forgot that conversation. I actually replay it in my mind often.

The day that followed was full of reviewing my demo tape, identifying what I needed to work on, meeting my new coworkers, and getting acclimated to being the face of an entire news station at 23. I co-anchored the morning show which meant that I had to be at the station at 3:30am to be ready for our show that aired at 4:30am. That meant that I had to check in with my producers, read the scripts for both shows, make sure that I was hair and makeup ready, and respond to emails/digital comments from viewers all before 4:00am. Whew!

Elaine invested a lot into my growth. I was fresh out of college and had no "real" formal training in broadcasting, so Elaine did whatever she could to ensure that I was ready for the big leagues. This time in my life was also when I was first introduced to just how mean the internet could be and how obsessive people become with public figures. Not always obsessive in a good way either. I was once followed home by a viewer. I began to receive several hateful messages detailing the way I spoke. Viewers said I spoke too fast, my words slurred, and that I sounded too country. The way I dressed and anything else in between was subject to their criticism. They would send these emails (that were only meant for be seen by me) to the entire newsroom. Can you imagine the embarrassment? I'm talking a newsroom of 30 people reading these terrible emails from strangers, literally ripping me to shreds. Normally, that would make me want to go harder and prove everyone wrong. Not this time though. I was defeated.

The station hired a talent coach named Stefania for me to work with weekly. Stefania would assign a list of homework every week. Sometimes that homework consisted of me going to the library and checking out 6 Dr. Seuss. I then had to read them in the mirror aloud every night. As silly as it sounds, it made my cadence and delivery on television a lot better. I also had to go to the mall to try on heels and walk around in them.

P.S. to this day I despise heels and I still can't really walk in them!

No matter how long Stefania and I worked together or how many quirky tricks she taught me to make be a better on-air personality, nothing seemed to work. The ratings for my morning show were falling, the terrible comments and emails were rolling in more than ever, and I was seriously struggling with depression.

One Friday as I was leaving work for the weekend, a viewer sent in an extremely detailed email listing all of the reasons why I needed to be fired and off of the air immediately. That was it. I was at my wit's end. The relationship that I was in was on the rocks, I was feuding with a once close family member, and I had just pulled a muscle (from carrying ridiculously heavy camera equipment – go figure!) so I was taking extremely heavy doses of Valium.

With all of these different factors going on in my life, I had no time for this insensitive troll and decided to give him a piece of my mind. I was fervently typing away when I received an email from the Sports anchor at our station:

I immediately stopped typing.

You know what this experience taught me? Negativity doesn't deserve a response. Ever.

To: Danielle Hughes ›

RE: Critique
Today at 3:20 PM

One thing I learned about this business, even the best have haters.

"If u ain't got No haters u ain't poppin" Keep up the good work!

PRO TIP 12

Not everything deserves a response. Especially, the haters. I try my best not to put too much energy into "haters" and "enemies" because in my world they don't exist. Truth is, there will ALWAYS be someone who has something to say about you. It's up to you to choose how you respond to those people. There was a point in my life where I responded to everything someone said to me. As I matured, I began to understand that silence is truly golden. Drake dropped a mixtape in 2009, and to this day it's probably one of my favorites. On one of the songs on that tape he says, "Diss me? You'll never hear a reply for it." I apply that to just about every factor of my life. I've heard the most ridiculously embarrassing and hurtful things about myself, and you know what I did? Nothing. Don't get me wrong, I am a firm believer in standing up for yourself, but if it costs you your peace in the process, it's too expensive. There are much more gratifying things to do in life than to prove your worth or talent to people who don't matter that much anyway. A wise man once told me, "You entertain a clown, you become a part of the circus." Choose your battles wisely, folks.

A QUICK NOTE ON NOT TAKING EVERYTHING PERSONALLY: I love 'The Four Agreements' by Don Miguel Ruiz. One of those agreements is: "Don't take anything personally." 9 times out of 10... the way that people treat you is a reflection of themselves... not you. If people can treat you vile and unkind, especially without knowing you, understand that is a direct reflection of their own insecurities and even jealousy. I have experienced people in my life who were afraid of my "light" and treated me harshly because of it. You never know what people are battling, and a lot of the time they like to project it onto you. Keep shining YOUR light, and don't take it personal.

The next few months following that day were seemingly worse and worse. I had no desire to go to work. I had no desire to make conversation with any of my coworkers. Heck, I had no desire to get out of the bed. I kept that bottle of Valium on my nightstand and contemplated downing the bottle one too many times.

That's when I knew something needed to change.

I was praying everyday and going to church every Sunday, but nothing seemed to fill my spirit. I tried my hardest to think back to a time where I was happy, but my mind continued to draw a blank. One Saturday evening, I heard a small still voice tell me to grab my vision board out of my closet. I hadn't looked at or even thought about it in months. I peeled myself out of bed and quickly snatched it off of the top shelf of my closet. As I stared at the board for what seemed to be hours, something began to click.

This was it. This was the feeling that I had been searching for.

In a moments time, all of those limiting beliefs that I had been battling about myself over the past few months instantly vanished. As I grazed my fingers over all of the meticulously placed affirmations, quotes, and photos that I cut and pasted, a sense of excitement came over me.

How can I teach people how to do this? I thought.

I've always been an educator at my core. I aim to educate in everything I do. I believe it's just in my veins. I decided that I wanted to teach people how to create vision boards. Not just any vision boards. Vision boards that work.

This is it! THIS is what I'm passionate about!

PRO TIP 13

Connect to your passion. I hadn't felt that on fire, or alive, for the sake of the matter in a long time. The Webster Dictionary's definition of passion goes a little something like this:

"*pas-sion:* strong and barely controllable emotion"

Well, The Danielle Dictionary definition goes like this: What will you do everyday without ever receiving a paycheck? That's your passion.

> When I was struggling to figure out what made me happy in life, I wrote down a list of things that I would do for free and still be satisfied with. If you're struggling to find your passion in life, I would suggest you do the same and make a list of things that make you happy... things that make you feel *alive!* Then, go from there. Whatever makes you feel on fire is directly connected to your purpose. That's what you were created to do. I don't believe that God put us on this earth to just pay bills and die. Figure out what lights you up and go do more of that.

Once I finally zeroed in on my passion. I went to work. I created a proposal and took it to the local library in my area to pitch my passion project: *"Oh, the places you'll go!"* A 4-part vision board series for young ladies aged 13-18. After a couple of meetings with the libraries executive board, they accepted the proposal and approved my use of the library for the next month for my program. I walked out of that meeting with a newfound sense of confidence. All of the worry and stress of the past few months was automatically stripped away. I hadn't experienced clarity like that in months, and I knew I never wanted to let that feeling go.

Meanwhile back at the ranch (AKA my job) things continued to quickly go up in flames. I operated as a zombie Monday through Friday from being so unfulfilled and lit up Friday evenings when I knew that the next morning I would be at the library assisting young people with creating the lives of their dreams through my vision board program.

April 1st, 2016. Elaine, called me into her office and sat

me down.

"The station is going through some changes and we're looking to move in a new direction." She firmly stated.

As unfulfilled and unhappy as I was at the station, for some strange reason I just knew that I was getting a promotion.

"You have 90 days, and you have to leave." Elaine continued.

"Is this a joke?" I questioned.

I mean… it was April Fools Day. My concern was valid.

"Unfortunately, Danielle, this is not a joke. Your performance has not been up to par, and we're looking for someone with more experience. You have 90 days from now, and your contract will end immediately." She concluded.

I was numb. Completely and utterly numb. I ran out of her office and into my car as tears began to fill my face.

Rewind to the beginning of this chapter:

"FIRED?!?! Again?!" I screamed while staring at my tear-filled face in my rearview mirror. I proceeded to call my mom and ask her what I was doing wrong in life. No matter how hard I tried, nothing seemed to work.

"These experiences will serve as an amazing testimony one day, Dani." My mom quietly whispered through the phone.

While all of that sounded great. I didn't understand how any of this madness would make any sense, let alone inspire anyone one day.

I went home that day and immediately fell to my knees and went into prayer. I don't remember exactly what that prayer consisted of, but I do remember ending it with "Let's get it."

And that's exactly what I did over the next 90 days.

I was immediately taken off of the morning show that I anchored and became the digital editor. This means that I basically re-posted stories and photos to the website for hours. While that was definitely a demotion and my embarrassment was hard to hide, I did my best to make that role my own.

By the end of May I knew that my stay in Georgia was slowly winding down. Writing became extremely therapeutic to me during this time, so I began to journal often. Here's an entry from May 2016:

5/28/16

Sooo… it's me again. Since we first talked my boss informed me that the station would not be renewing my contract because she was not seeing the "growth" that she expected to see. I was so uninspired in that position, but I am SO grateful for this moment. I know that God is going to really reveal himself through this new transition… I didn't want to stay in news forever and I guess He saw fit and opened that door for me early. I now know the true meaning of dedication, leadership, and hard work. I'm looking forward to what God has planned. I know it's going to blow my mind.

I was trying my best to see the positive in a situation that provided me so much negative evidence. The lease on my apartment would be up in 60 days, and I needed to figure something out… and *fast*. I had no intentions on moving back to Detroit so I applied to at least 35 jobs in Georgia with the hopes that I would be contacted by one.

To make a long story short: I never heard back from any of those jobs. Actually, I did hear back from one, but they said I wasn't what they were looking for. Whatever.

After careful consideration, and wise counsel from my Mom, (… *actually, it was all my Mom because if it wasn't for her logic I would probably be somewhere in Atlanta living on the streets looking for work)* I ended up packing whatever I could into my Ford Focus, and with the help of my parents, shipped it back to Michigan. I purchased a one-way flight back to Detroit and began to mentally prepare myself for what was to come. I hadn't lived in Detroit in close to 5 years, and I was not at all excited about moving back.

I dreaded this day for a long time. However, on my official last day at the news station, I woke up with the supernatural peace that only God could provide. I walked into the station, gave Elaine a hug, and thanked her for all she had done. I walked to the "Wall of Fame" where my official headshot had been hanging for months, took a deep breath, and removed the photo from the wall.

Walking out of the station for the last time, the air felt different. The sun shined a little brighter, and the blue skies seemed to be just a bit bluer. I looked up to the sky and smiled.

Let's get it.

PRO TIP 14

Keep it moving. I always try to keep this quote in mind when I'm at a crossroad in life:

"Success seems to be connected with action. Successful people keep moving. They make mistakes, but they don't quit."

Please keep this in mind when you are faced with dilemmas or hard decisions of any kind. I believe that you should first consult with yourself and whatever higher power that you identify with, but the next step is to definitely stay in motion. When you become stagnant, you literally become stuck – in real life. If you keep it moving, you are destined to land where you need to be. As human beings, we are just huge balls of energy. All of our actions and reactions are energetic, and you will receive exactly what you exert. Rest and relaxation are essential to taking care of your body but losing momentum during crunch time could be detrimental to your progress. Taking one small step each day in the right direction is better than not moving at all. After all, "a body in motion stays at motion." Keep going.

PRO TIP RECAP:

#10 – TRUST YOUR INSTINCTS

#11 – BE GRATEFUL FOR THE RE-ROUTE

#12 – NOT EVERYTHING DESERVES A RESPONSE

#13 – CONNECT WITH YOUR PASSION

#14 – KEEP IT MOVING

Based off the tips in this chapter, how do you plan to bounce back?

1.)

2.)

3.)

Notes

Notes

PRINCIPLE: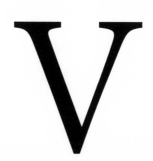

Stay Ready (so you don't

have to get ready)

"Switched hustles…

been killin' em ever since."

–Young Jeezy

By August 2016, I was settling into my new life. I had just officially moved back in with my parents and immediately began plotting on the next move. I'm not sure about you, but there's something about almost being at rock bottom that motivates me like no other. I was now unemployed with a daily schedule of: nothing.

When I was younger, my mom would always say "an idle mind is the devil's playground," and this is VERY true… if you let it. With all of my newfound downtime, I could've easily fell victim to my circumstances and wallowed in my sorrow, but I decided to take control instead. I wanted to **create** instead of **wait.**

I used this time to read. A lot. I knew that life would one day pick back up again, and I wouldn't have as much leisure time, so I soaked up as much game as I could through reading. I've always loved to read but I began to use it as a coping mechanism while living in Georgia and working in TV News. Once I started to feel myself sinking into a depressive state, I would read 15 pages of a book a day to keep my mind sharp. One of the books that helped me through that time, besides my Bible, is the 48 Laws of Power by Robert Greene. Law 25 talks about the importance of recreating yourself:

"Do not accept that society foists on you. Re-create yourself by forging a new identity, one that commands attention and never bores the audience. Be the master of your own image rather than letting others define it for you." –Robert Greene

It was time that I did just that. I was becoming a new person and shedding all of the mistakes of the past.

Since I hadn't lived in Detroit for some years, I had to

get acclimated with the new community around me. Since I had so much free time and a new sense of purpose, I made a list of things that I loved to do and would continuously do if I never received a paycheck for them. At the top of that list was "teach young people how to find and create their purpose in life."

After getting clear on what it was that I was passionate about, I reached out to everyone who I felt could assist me in getting closer to this dream of working with young people. By this time, the nonprofit that I co-founded was up and running so I hustled to get the programming in schools in Detroit. My days consisted of meeting after meeting with school administrators, educators, and associates who worked with youth in some capacity. I was chasing a dream that no one else could see... one that made me absolutely no money but made me happy. At that moment, happiness was all that I wanted. During this time, I probably spoke to over 500 students in metro Detroit just to be in the midst of possibility to create the type of reality that I wanted to experience everyday. I'm sure I looked utterly ridiculous to everyone else. I saw the light at the end of the tunnel though. I believe that made all the difference. Thus, my association with being "the girl on the news" started to cease, and I reemerged as a community change agent, or Chief Changemaker as I like to call myself. Most importantly, I became an advocate for youth in the city of Detroit.

PRO TIP 15

Recreate yourself. When I moved back home and decided that I was ready to pursue my purpose full time, I began to shed multiple layers. One of those layers was my identity. For the longest, I was associated with being in news. Well, after being fired twice from two different television stations it was obvious that I needed to make a change. After being intentional about finding what I was passionate about, I knew it was time to confidently walk into my new purpose. Earlier in this chapter, I talked about Law 25 in The 48 Laws of Power: "Recreate Yourself." This doesn't mean just physically, but internally and spiritually as well. What are you currently clinging to that is holding you back from recreating yourself? Whatever it is, let it go, and step into the destiny that God has for you. It doesn't matter what anyone has to say about you. What do YOU say about you? That's most important. In the next year, you won't be the same person that you are now. So, why should you appear that way? You can recreate yourself in a plethora of ways. It just depends on what resonates best with you. Every new level of your life will demand a different version of growth. I've learned that it's a lot harder to transition to your next level while clinging to your old self and old habits. Don't be afraid to recreate yourself... over and over and over again.

ADVICE FROM A PRO: Jade Ulmer, CEO of Luxx Media Group

Branding has become so critically important in the building of your company, but I believe it is extremely necessary to brand not only your business, but yourself as well. With over 6 years of experience in marketing and branding, I've realized that majority of your potential clients will ultimately buy into the company's owner before the actual company itself. It may seem uncomfortable or awkward at first, but my income has doubled since taking that next to transparently tell my personal story. Your potential customers want to see who they are spending money with! They want to feel connected and personable with you as well as relatable. You are just as important as the product and/or service you offer, and you could be missing out on strategic opportunities that could change your life. People do business with those they trust so it's important to create a lasting positive impression on your potential clients. Providing the transparency that people desire and becoming familiar with your brand's purpose can open unimaginable doors for you and your company. Did you know by branding yourself, you are becoming an asset to your company, while also enhancing your brands image as well? You are providing an opportunity for your customers to know you, what you stand for, and what your brand can offer them. You will also find that your personal brand can become more valuable than your company itself with the proper brand strategies. Yes, it may be safer to play a behind the scenes role for your brand but think about all the possibilities and opportunities you can receive by being your true authentic self. I'm so glad I decided to make the transition to incorporating my personal image into my brand. Remember that you are a walking billboard! After all, if you cannot sell yourself it may be even harder to sell your products!

IG: @IAmJadeRenee I www.luxxmedia.com

I made sure that I hustled for everything that I desired during this time period. I didn't have an actual plan of what I wanted to do, but I figured if I just kept working towards it, God would handle the rest.

With little to no resources (and my unemployment check,) I hosted an event for Detroit youth in 2016 in collaboration with a local nonprofit organization named The Neema Project. The event was titled: "The Next Level" and that was exactly what we aimed to do. We wanted to connect young people in our city with mentors to get them to the next level. The event ended up becoming a major success. We served several youth and their parents that day and provided them with the resources to make their dreams a reality.

During that event, one of my colleagues asked me if I was familiar with a nonprofit based out of New York called, "The Future Project." I had never heard of it.

"You're a Dream Director!" he excitedly chanted.

A what?

He began to explain how Dream Directors were national change makers placed in schools across the country to inspire young people to discover their passions and purpose. He continued to tell me that the application for the program would be opening soon and that I should apply. I immediately took down the information. I began to read more and more about the organization and fell in love with the mission and their ideals. That same night, I printed out a photo of their logo and pasted it to my vision board.

8 months later I became a Dream Director.

I get to do what I love every single day with youth in my hometown, and I'm *paid* for it. I believe that all of this came about by doing the work.

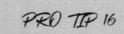

PRO TIP 16

I believe that when God sees you doing your part, He will multiply what it is that you're asking for. I know that He's done it for me and will do it for you, too. No matter how many vision boards you make, nothing will actually happen if you don't get out and work towards it. Make just ONE step towards your goal each day. Just one. That new position you've been praying for? Do your research and begin preparing for the interview. Ready to purchase a home? Start working on your credit and saving money to prepare for your new lifestyle as a homeowner. Want to learn how to cook? Begin trying new recipes once a week to get a knack for it. Faith without action doesn't mean much. Do the work.

Back when I moved to Atlanta for college, (remember with just $800) I knew that I was ready to take myself seriously as a young professional. I went through some type of metamorphosis during that summer, and I immediately wanted to activate my new "grown woman" status. I had no professional photos to use for pitches or to send to employers. I had no business cards and no clue what a LinkedIn was. I consistently did my research and decided all of that was going to change. I was tired of having to let go of opportunities just because I didn't have the basics.

Around this time, one of the hottest celebrity photographers in Atlanta was running a photoshoot special for $150. Now, keep in mind that I only had $800 to my name – probably less – and it wouldn't make sense to blow that much money on photos. So, guess what I did?! I purchased the photos anyway.

Those photos were my first official "headshots" and believe it or not, 7 years later, I'm still using them. Investing in quality will always give you the greatest ROI. It may have seemed like a lot of money at the time, but it definitely paid off.

Next, I logged onto vistaprint.com and created myself a business card template. I'm pretty sure that cost me around 20 bucks for 400 cards. I also made myself a LinkedIn profile that night. I had no actual reason to be doing all of these things, but I wanted to make sure that I was prepared when opportunities began to come about.

Just like that, I had new professional photos, biz cards (they were basic, but they served their purpose,) and a new site that explained who I was as a "freelance student journalist." I was actually just a kid at Georgia State who was trying to figure out what she wanted to do with her life, but that title sounded nice and fancy so I ran with it. As a result, I ended up catching the eye of a publicist who represented a few up and coming actors and artists in Atlanta. I had done a little background research on her, so I was prepared to shoot my shot and ask if she was looking for interns. I did just that, and to my surprise she said that she was actually looking for two new interns at the moment.

I proceeded to give her my information: my sleek new LinkedIn profile detailed my recent articles (it was actually just random articles I wrote to have some content), my new "adult" headshots, and my business cards. Two days later, I was chosen for the internship!

Now, I didn't get paid, but I wasn't expecting to. I was seeking the experience, and that's exactly what I got. The skills that I received from working with that agency led me to a paid internship with the top-rated TV news station in Atlanta, a job as a news anchor at 23 in the same state, and now - my name on the Forbes list.

Not sure how all of that is connected? I'll tell you.

PRO TIP 17

Promote yourself. No one is going to represent you better than you can. Want to be treated as a professional? Present yourself as one! People will take you seriously when they see that you take yourself and your personal brand seriously. Don't think that you have a personal brand? Well, you do.

Everyone does. It's what people say about you when you're not around. Don't be the person who is known as sloppy and unprofessional because they don't have the basics in tact. You wouldn't believe how many "businesses" I come into contact with that sell products or services with no website or no way to contact them. In this day and age that's totally unacceptable! We have access to so much information and entirely too many resources for you not to have simple things like a professional headshot and a LinkedIn. I keep referencing this because before I had a personal website, I had a LinkedIn profile which served its purpose just as well. Did I mention it's free? When I moved back home from Detroit after working in news, I wanted to make sure that people knew about the work that was being done with Detroit youth through my nonprofit. I couldn't afford a publicist, so I became my own. I researched local media outlets, learned how to make a press release, stayed consistent, followed up after two weeks if I didn't hear anything, and voila! We landed our first TV interview in Detroit to promote our first big event. Put yourself out there, and never be afraid to promote yourself, your business, or anything else that your name is attached to. No matter what that looks like for you, make sure that you're confident and *consistent*. That makes a world of difference.

I'm sure you've heard the phrase, "stay ready so you don't have to get ready." If you haven't already been living by this phrase, I suggest you start now. Staying ready can mean a lot of things. Do you update your resume every so often in case a new opportunity presents itself? Do you make sure that your social media profiles are up to date with your recent activities? Is the domain for your website on a reoccurring payment? Nothing is worse than going to someone's business site and seeing that it's expired. No bueno. All of these instances play a key factor in making sure that you're always ready.

I haven't "needed" a resume since 2016. I still update my resume bi-monthly, though. Why? Because you never know when someone may unexpectedly ask you for it. You never know when that big break you've been praying for will just automatically fall out of the sky and into your lap. Make sure you're prepared for it.

ADVICE FROM A PRO: Bee Brown, Owner and Lead Publicist of The Bee Agency

The understanding of having a firm foundation laid for your business is key in scaling and growing your business. This also helps when you've reached the point of being able to share your story on a local or national level, and there's no question if you're ready to show off your brand house. Having a proper brand foundation laid helps not only with keeping you organized, but aids in the mindset of staying ready, so you don't have to get ready.

The Blueprint: This can also serve as your business plan or overview goals you set for yourself and your brand. This can include, achievable client measures, accounting, and legal matters such as trademarking, LLC/ S-Corp, etc.

This is a very important piece of the foundation process that I skipped over, and now I'm backtracking. An important piece of laying your blueprint is protecting your intellectual property. This is where trademarking comes in to play. This is also the point where registering your business with your state and federal government is crucial in order for you to file taxes and open a business bank account.

The Framework: This includes the brand identity + coaching of your brand. Don't let the word branding take you to the thought of colors, logos, and font. This process is when you invest in a candid coaching session with a brand coach.

Also, develop the framework to understanding your lane. This is when you develop the understanding of your target/ focus areas, niche, and firm expertise. You may change this as your brand grows and expands. In my own journey, I had to re-frame my focus and carve out my lane, which helped me lay my foundation.

The Design: This is the fun part; the development of your brand look that includes logo, website, visuals and brand content. When investing in the design aspect of your brand, it's important to work with a designer that holds education key in their branding agency.

When investing in your design package, it's important to not only learn throughout the process, but build a lasting relationship with your designer, to keep everything consistent. I would highly recommend working with a credible brand that not only designs, but codes as well.

The Open House: This is when you have your brand house ready for show and tell with a Marketing/Public Relations plan in place. They will act as your "real estate" agent while introducing you and your business to the world.

This is the phase when it should feel like your brand is coming together and ready to present to the world. There may be setbacks and changes, but it's all apart of laying your foundation and trusting the process.

Take your time laying out your foundation and hold the understanding that the process takes time. Laying the foundation is key to creating a solid blueprint to your forever growing brand. There is an understanding needed in order for you to tell your story while introducing your brand to the world. Within this understanding is the firm foundation of your business from top to bottom.

IG: @BeeBrownPR I www.thebeeagency.com

PRO TIP 18

THE STAY READY CHECKLIST

Are you ready? Check the boxes below to make sure!

Your name and personal brand will outlive any employer or current place in life. I've added a checklist below to help you lay the foundation. This list is in no particular order. Check them off as you grow and build!

☐ Register or update your first and last name with every major social media site. If you have a business or non-profit, make sure you're doing the same using your business name.

☐ Buy your personal domain name. (ex: danielledhughes. com) GoDaddy makes it super easy to do this.

☐ Ask 5 people that you trust what they would pay you for or what they believe you're in an expert in.

☐ Find out who your target audience is.

☐ Get professional photos taken. (EVERY professional needs a professional headshot!)

☐ Create a clear and concise mission statement for yourself and your brand.

☐ Get a personalized email address (ex: hello@danielledhughes. No more Gmail, Yahoo or AOL addresses!)

☐ Create your logo.

☐ Design and print custom business cards.

☐ Create an email list to further engage with your audience and potential and current clients.

☐ Create a consistent content strategy. Whatever you do.

STAY   CONSISTENT.

- [ ] Select a legal structure (ex: Sole Proprietorship, Partnership, Limited Liability Company, Corporation or S-Corporation.)

- [ ] Write a business plan.

- [ ] Obtain your Federal Employer Identification Number (your   businesses' Social Security Number.)

- [ ] Open a business account.

- [ ] Invest in branding.

- [ ] Market yourself as if your life depends on it. Always remember, the best marketer wins!

- [ ] TRADEMARK, TRADEMARK, TRADEMARK!

PRO TIP RECAP

PRO TIP #15 – RECREATE YOURSELF

PRO TIP # 16 – DO THE WORK

PRO TIP #17 – PROMOTE YOURSELF

PRO TIP #18 – STAY READY SO YOU DON'T HAVE TO GET READY

Based off the tips in this chapter, how will you stay ready?

1.)

2.)

3.)

Notes

Notes

PRINCIPLE: VI

Gratitude is the Attitude

"Gratitude can transform common days into thanksgivings, turn routine jobs into joy, and change ordinary opportunities into blessings."

–William Arthur Ward

Regardless of my personal views behind the history of Thanksgiving, I find it amazing that we have an entire day dedicated to being thankful in the United States. I also find it fascinating that as human beings, we put more emphasis on what we don't have, than we do expressing gratitude for what we do have.

Several research studies have been completed to show that the act of gratitude can improve your performance in work and life, your mood, your surroundings, and your mental and emotional states.

Simply put, the definition of gratitude is, "the quality of being thankful; readiness to show appreciation for and to return kindness."

Earlier in this book, I mentioned how practicing gratitude drastically changed the course of my life over the last year.

In January 2017, I set the intention that I was going to become a better person. I was fed up with myself and knew that the internal work that I was NOT doing was in direct correlation with how things were playing out with my life.

I immediately grabbed my blush pink daily planner and began to scribble away. I made a list of 5 things that I wanted to work on in the coming year. That list went as follows:

- TITHING (Money & Time)

- SAVING (Money & Time)

- BEING NON JUDGEMENTAL

- GIVING

- MORE GENEROSITY

I started working on this list one by one, in both my daily interactions with people and within myself. As simple as this list seems, it was a lot more difficult to actually put these principles into practice.

I began to see an extreme difference in myself and my life once I started being mindful about what type of energy I wanted to put into the atmosphere. I challenge you to begin expressing insane gratitude for what you have (and don't have) in your life. Once you change your mindset to believing that EVERYTHING is working in your favor, you'll understand that even the things that don't feel good are still meant for your greater good.

I gifted my mom a "Gratitude Journal" this Christmas and asked that she write down three things that she's grateful for each day. I believe that we become so engulfed in what goes wrong with our day that we never take the time to reflect on all of the things that have gone right.

So, let's start now.

List 3 things that you're grateful for RIGHT NOW. This doesn't take any deep thought. Just think about the top 3 things that you're grateful for in this very moment.

Ready... set... GO!

#GratitudeChallenge

1) _____

2) _____

3) _____

Every day try your best to pick out the top 3 things that you appreciate and are excited or grateful for. You can use a specific notebook, or you can use the blank pages in this book to use as your very own Gratitude Journal.

It also helps to stop putting so much emphasis on what we are *unhappy* about and start focusing on the things that we want and are happy about. Try it and watch how life changes.

The point that I'm trying to make with this is that you will see a sudden improvement in your mood, health, and several other areas by simply choosing to adjust your mindset and call it all joy.

PRO TIP 19

Show gratitude for your life. You woke up this morning! That's something to be grateful for. You're reading this book! You have vision to see. Honestly, if you're breathing, it's a blessing. Let's show more appreciation for the small things this year and watch how they avalanche into bigger blessings.

Here are some ways that I'm working on showing gratitude for my life. Hope they'll resonate with you, too!

- **Make eye contact with people:** A very simple gesture, but it's a way to show that you're present and in the moment.

- Patience is a virtue: LITERALLY. I understand it isn't everyone's ministry but putting in a concentrated effort to exercise your patience is a game changer. Remember we're all dealing with personal struggles that no one knows about. Be kind and patient!

- Be gracious: Exercising graciousness, especially during life's challenges is a game changer. Life comes in waves, so you will definitely be thrown curve balls. Be sure to handle them with grace. Not only does it strengthen your faith muscles, but it makes you more mindful as well.

- Share your time, treasure or talents: You never know how you can bless someone just by using the gifts that you've been naturally given.

- Apologize: We all get upset, and our personal egos can make us feel like we're always right and never make mistakes. That's probably the furthest thing from the truth. Be willing to apologize to the ones you love (and the ones you don't.) A little compromise can go a long way in a relationship.

- Smile: Smiles are contagious, and they make you feel better no matter what mood you're in. They also make others feel better, too. No matter the season you're currently in, smile through it. It will pass. It always does.

ADVICE FROM A PRO: Toni Jones, Wellness Strategist and Founder of Wife Comma

Gratitude as a Tool to Manifest Your Dreams

Tool #1 Gratitude as a Coping Tool

When pursuing your dreams, you are guaranteed several hiccups, challenges, plot twists, and sometimes traumas and heartbreaks. When life brings these interesting visitors into our dream pursuit path, we must have tools to access so we can cope when these plot twists show up in our life. From your cell phone cracking, to losing a job, to a romantic distraction. No matter the scenario, we must be able to hold space for our feelings without compromising our commitment to our dreams. So, this is how you can practice gratitude as a coping tool:

When challenges arise, you must first say, "Thank you. I am looking forward to the solution and releasing the discomfort of this." Another statement you can use is "Thank you for coming, what are you here to teach me? I don't like how you feel, but I receive the blessing, lessons and growth that I am to gain from you" This is literally a hacker when it comes to your mental and emotional processing because it removes you from the conditional victim response, believing life is happening to you, instead of believing life is happening for you.

Here are some other gratitude statements that you can speak out… (and yes, you can cry while you speak them):

"Pain and discomfort is in service to my growth, awareness, dopeness, expansion, dreams, and abundance."

"I know this doesn't feel good, and I really hoped this wouldn't be my now right now, but I receive the good that wishes to come from these challenges."

"I surrender to these problems that come from my good choices. I will prove that I want my dream more than I want to glorify this temporary discomfort."

"I am so grateful that I can feel my whole life while I pursue and manifest my dreams, like I feel all of it."

Remember that in order for you to live your dreams and a life you love, you must be able to cope in life because there will be many tests that come your way. You've gotta stay ready to equip yourself to past those tests.

Tool #2 Gratitude as a Manifesting Generator Tool

Some say the universe lovvvvessss gratitude. Gratitude is the dessert of manifesting because it is the sweetest and fastest way to manifest what you are dreaming of. Manifesting your dreams is all about taking what is in your mind and giving it the energy to empower it to transition from your mental reality into your physical reality. So, think of gratitude as the ultimate energetic generator to manifesting. What does this look like? I am glad that you asked. Here are some practical ways to implementing gratitude as your manifesting generating tool.

Activity One:

Step 1: Write down 3 things you desire, but "feel" like you are lacking.

Step 2: Next, write down the emotions you feel that come from that sense of lack.

Step 3: Lastly, write down those three things in a gratitude statement, including how it makes you feel to have those three things.

EX:// I am not smart with my money and income, and I don't have enough money.

Transformed into a gratitude belief statement: I am so grateful for the self awareness that I have about how I can grow and evolve in how I manage my money in the healthiest way that benefits me long term.

Activity Two:

Step 1: Turn those three things into an affirmation.

Step 2: Repeat this affirmation three times a day 3 times day.

Step 3: Write this affirmation down everyday.

Activity Three:

Gratitude Affirmative statements to say as a morning ritual

1. I am believing and growing into my natural ability as manifesting generator because I am attracting who I am in every way.

2. I know that what I appreciate appreciates. I know what I focus on the most I attract more of. I am grateful and appreciative for what I have now in this reality, and this fuels me receiving more of it"

3. "I am grateful for..." Get extensive with this list. Create a vision board of gratitude and add more to it each week or month.

Tool # 3 Gratitude as a Healing Tool

We all know that mindset is the key to attracting and manifesting your dream life, right? We have been hearing that so much, and it very much is true. But, we must consider the heart set as well- meaning our emotional and feeling world. The internal habitat of our dreams is our mind and heart, and we must be aware of what the internal world needs for nourishment. Our mind and heart are an accumulation of our memories and early experiences with our care-givers and peers, etc. This includes pain, heart break, and disappointment. Therefore, by the time we are adults and active some level of consciousness and awareness of what we want in our life and we will have to heal our minds and hearts to start creating that dream life. Now this dream life is not measured by society standards. We are talking about that inner voice that says there is more. The one that says, "I want to live not just my best life, but my most authentic life." So, let's talk about what healing your internal habitat of your dreams.

When it comes to your mindset through gratitude

Throwback Practice | Track down your earliest memories of believing you are not being enough... when you first felt scarcity and lack. Think about when you felt financial limits were apart of life.

Then get present with those memories and speak to your version of yourself that felt and experienced that. Next tell yourself, "Thank you for feeling and processing our experiences. I am here now to take from here. We don't have to believe in this anymore let me show you what the truth is..."

When it comes to your heart set you must know what makes you feel good and what doesn't make you feel good because emotional energy is essential to manifesting. Therefore, healing your heart from the experiences and fears that may have power over your dreams coming forth is preciously important.

Essentially, what you appreciate appreciates. This means that the better you feel about a thing, the more you are present with what is. Focusing your perception on the good of what is now allows universe to feed you more good.

Gratitude is a way of drawing more into your life to be grateful for. Just like in your body you have a nervous system and other complex systems that keep the body in operation. Gratitude is apart of the spiritual body to keep manifesting in operation. Gratitude matters, so make it matter in your life so you can create the life you deserve, love, and dream about.

IG: @WifeComma I www.wifecomma.com

My personal slogan (and Instagram bio) for the last 5 years has read: "A lover of God, good novels, and good manners." That is a quote from a book titled Gentlewoman by Enitan Bereola.

The older I get, I truly see how mindfulness has played a role in my growth. This is a concept that I've recently been introduced to, but I've made it a staple in my daily interaction with others.

Mindfulness is nothing more or less than the quality or state of being conscious or aware of something. We all operate with some sort of mindfulness in our everyday interactions with others. We do so just by taking the time to slow down and pay closer attention to how we're moving throughout our day.

Here are a few of the ways I've strengthened my mindfulness this year:

Take 10 minutes after my morning routine to sit and do nothing.

I like to take these 10 minutes to just be and set my intention for the day. This may include listening to some calming music as well. If you have super high active days, it helps to take several minutes throughout the day to center and re-focus.

Stay aware of my breathing.

I was once a staunch yoga enthusiast. (Well, after my first couple of classes I got over that rather quickly.) Yoga may not be my preferred relaxation method, but it taught me a lot about my breathing. Concentrating on your breathing can sound like a piece of cake until you actually take the time to do it. If your mind races a million miles a minute like mine, then it can take more work to actually calm down your thoughts to focus on your breathing. Ultimately, doing this practice helps you to drown out your thoughts to focus on the present.

Meditate.

Meditating doesn't have to be a well thought out ceremonious occasion with candles, incense, and yoga mats, but rather a few minutes of your day to sit down, focus on your breathing and reflect. From my experience, I've found my mood to be much better after taking a few minutes to meditate. There are several guided meditations (voiceover included) on the internet if you need some help getting started.

Mind Your Manners

As my Instagram bio boasts, I am actually a lover of good manners. I appreciate small phrases like "please" and "thank you," or even polite gestures to show that you're respectful and considerate of others' feelings.

Last summer, I watched the well-known Netflix documentary: *What the Health*. Like most of America, I was immediately turned off and jumped head first into a vegan diet. Not only was it significantly better for the environment, but I saw a drastic change in my energy and clarity almost immediately. I was spending the summer in New York (one of the vegan hubs of America) for a training and figured that I would be able to keep up my newfound lifestyle with ease once I returned to Detroit.

Well, that didn't happen.

What *did* happen was I decided to become a pescatarian. I found that jumping into a diet and eliminating basically all of the foods that I had been eating for 25 years was not the move and would take a lot more work than what I was willing to put in at the time. Thanks to one of my Sister Friends, Toni, I immersed myself into a full lifestyle makeover (mind, body, and spirit) and I can honestly say that it has been one of the most transformative times of my life thus far.

Life gets hectic. We all know that to be true. The best way to shield depression, disease and unnecessary drama within your body is to simply take care of it. Now, I'm no health guru, but I am committed to leading a healthy lifestyle which requires shedding everything that I was accustomed to eating and doing while growing up.

It is my hope that you're taking care of your body. After all, we only get one and if we take care of it – it will surely take care of us. Your body was created to protect you, so please do your very best to treat it as the temple that it is.

I have created a simple 'Get Yo' Life' checklist for you to refer to when life gets hectic and you need to get yourself back on track!

GET YO' LIFE CHECKLIST

1. Drink at least 5-7 liters of water per day.

2. Eat your fruit daily and something green with every meal (or at least per day.)

3. Get some fresh air.

4. Find small ways to stay active/exercise throughout the day.

5. Practice mindfulness each day.

6. Take at least 5-10 minutes to yourself to breathe and regroup daily.

7. Make sure you're getting 6-8 hours of sleep per night.

8. Tell the truth and set boundaries for yourself.

9. Ditch your phone for at least an hour each day.

10. Celebrate your small wins daily.

11. Visit trained physicians often. (Doctors, Dentists, Optometrists, Dermatologists, etc.) None of the above will matter if you're not seeking professional help to make sure you're on the right track! You'll feel so much better once you do.

This past summer, I traveled to Nairobi, Kenya on a Mission trip with several other global educators. Together we embarked on an 8-day trek across the country to assist with the building of a library at a local elementary school.

While on that trip, the group I was with was robbed at gunpoint. All of their belongings were taken from them by masked men with rifles and machetes. Just 20 minutes prior, I was with the group in one of the rental properties we were staying in, celebrating another one of our colleague's birthdays.

I happened to leave the group because my cousin texted me saying that she needed me to call her ASAP. She was back home in the States at the time, so I figured that whatever she needed was an emergency and required my attention. I immediately left the guest home to call her back. After trying to reach her a few times to no avail, I decided not to return to the other guest house where the party was taking place, but to prepare for bed instead. Not even 20 minutes later, I was awakened out of my sleep to an extremely loud knock at the door. Seconds later the door burst open. It was the police alerting me that my colleagues were just robbed at gunpoint, and that we needed to evacuate the premises immediately.

In a frantic rush, I grabbed what I could and hurried out of the door. That night consisted of fervent prayers, piercing screams, anguish and a lot of unanswered questions amongst our group.

How could something like this happen so far from home? We came here to share our time and talents with a country in need and this is how it ends? We were sent to the airport with not much information or closure and began our individual journeys back home. In the heat of the moment, I don't think that I recognized just how much distress or trauma this one incident had caused me. Once back home, I could not sleep nor eat for weeks. I would sleep 2 hours or so a night and wake right up. I would think that I was hearing noises of someone trying to break in all throughout the night. I even created a makeshift fort in front of my front door to block any intruders trying to enter my home. Sounds silly, right? Well, I thought it was silly too, but it's the only way I felt safe. I would literally feel like I was being followed everywhere I went. Even though I wasn't, my mind was creating stories for me and I was believing them. I prayed day and night for these feelings and thoughts to be stripped away from me, but deep down I knew that I needed an intervention.

It wasn't until I consulted one of my closest friends, Erin, to express how I was feeling that I received a breakthrough. Erin had just completed her Master's program in Psychology and was on the way to completing her doctorate. I knew that she would have an answer for me.

"You need to go to therapy…"

Now, I was no stranger to therapy. I first began seeing a therapist at the tender age of 8. My cousin had recently committed suicide, and I was taking it pretty hard. So much so, that I would urinate myself if no one agreed to take me to the bathroom because I feared being alone that much.

I was pulled out of my 3rd grade classroom one day by a woman I had never seen before. She assured me that she was there to help me, but I was super apprehensive. The woman took me by the hand and explained that she was the school therapist. I was told that my Mom got in contact with her because she was worried and wanted to help me. The woman went on to ask if I knew what trauma was. I immediately shook my head because I had never even heard the word before. She explained that I was traumatized by my cousin's sudden death and that my body was now reacting to it. I would begin to see her weekly after that initial session. I became more and more comfortable with her as the weeks went on, and we ultimately began to form a bond. I have not seen or heard from that woman in years, but I do know her guidance and care helped me get through that rough patch at such a young age.

I would return to therapy 7 years later at the age of 15 for an altercation with a family member that left me badly bruised: physically and emotionally. It was my Mom who suggested that I go back to therapy again because of the aftermath of what could and *would* happen if I didn't address those feelings. I'm so grateful for her quick action in those moments because if I didn't get help, who knows where I would be.

So, there I was back in therapy for the 3rd time looking for some sort of closure. While I thought that I was going for the incident that happened in Kenya, I began bringing up all types of unresolved feelings from an old romantic relationship that I couldn't shake, to childhood experiences that I never quite dealt with. After our sessions came to an end, I knew for a fact that I needed to make therapy a part of my everyday life. The clarity that I received after each session began to change me from the inside out. I now knew how to deal with certain situations and understand that everything happening to me was actually happening for me as well. I started sleeping and eating regularly again, and I regained my confidence to where I no longer felt as though I was being followed. My therapist played a huge role in that. I'm grateful.

PRO TIP 22

Self-care is much more than massages. I know that the self-care fad has become increasingly popular in the last few years, but it's much more than fancy spa days. TRUE care is making sure that you're in top shape: mentally, physically and spiritually. Listen to your mind and body and adhere to the signs that it gives you. Self-care comes in the form of therapy, detoxing, meditation, solitude and more. Whatever it looks like to you, just make sure that you're allotting time for it. You will see, and most importantly, FEEL the difference. Your future self will thank you!

HER STORY: Erin A. White, MA, TLLP, PsyD Student

Oftentimes, humans do not like to face the reality that everything will not always be okay. However, it is not until we admit an issue exists that a solution can be formed. I believe everyone should utilize some form of therapy because we will all experience adversity at least once in our lives. It is a misconception that if you go to therapy, there must be something seriously wrong. However, the individuals that are strong enough to attend therapy are demonstrating a mental toughness that most do not possess. People also believe that if you bury a problem, the problem goes away. This is also flawed thinking because you can never get over something, you can only work through it. If you attempt to bury your feelings and emotions, they will only build up until one day they come to a head. I know this to be true due to both personal and professional experiences. Most of the clients I have worked with thus far were in therapy because they had reached a breaking point.

Coming from a family full of mental health professionals, my career path was almost hand selected for me. Although my family members with experience advised me to pursue a different path due to the stress that comes along with the profession, I chose to follow my heart and my passion. I plan to dedicate my career to combat the negative stigma of mental health in the African-American community. I grew up in a home with a single mother due to my father's struggle with substance abuse. My father was present in my life despite his addiction. My mother never spoke ill of my father and sheltered me from most negative experiences. However, she raised me to be strong and empathic to others' experiences. I cannot say that I had a difficult upbringing, however, I am aware that the absence of affection has affected personal relationships throughout my life. I was also expected to be an exceptional student and to excel in everything I attempted. While I do believe it is important to set high expectations for your children, it is also important to let them know it is okay to fail, because without failure there is no achievement.

My mother and her siblings were raised by a single mother who also taught them to be strong. Strength is an attribute most African-American caregivers strive to instill in their young due to the hardships our community has endured throughout our history. However, while strength is instilled, there is an overwhelming absence of vulnerability. While my mother always encouraged me to be open about how I was feeling, I always wanted to be strong just like her. Therefore, I hid a lot of my true feelings about the absence of my father and sometimes my struggles in school. A number of individuals have an innate fear of being vulnerable. Therefore, we shy away from being completely open and honest with feelings and emotions that force us to be vulnerable. Now, as a 26-year-old psychotherapist, I have come to realize the abnormalities in that way of thinking.

I would not be where I am today without the guidance and encouragement from my parents, and for them I am forever grateful. I know that my mother raised me to be strong, because in this world nothing is handed to you. I work hard each day knowing that if my father won the fight against his addiction, I can achieve whatever it is I set my mind to. With this, I also realize that there is nothing wrong with extra help. Therefore, I sought out my own personal therapy.

Throughout my life, I have set high expectations for myself because I was raised to be the best and to do my best. Therefore, I never really gave myself room for mistakes. This mindset worked for me until I reached a point in my life where I was unsure of the direction I would like to take. I have never been a fan of change or uncertainty, and this would prove to be my breaking point. By deciding to go to therapy, I was able to acknowledge that life is not perfect, and that I can make mistakes. It allowed me to be more transparent with my own clients and normalize their experience. I am able to encourage my family and friends to go to therapy, and I do my best to check on my loved ones because you never know what a person may be going through.

For anyone that may read this contribution and decide it is time to reach out for help, know there are many resources available to you. For individuals struggling with addiction, MyAddiction.com is an excellent resource. For African-American women searching for someone who may be able to relate closely to their experience, therapyforblackgirls.com houses a directory of therapists in your area. Additionally, Psychology Today houses a directory for all therapies in your local area. I am so happy that the tides are changing slowly but surely concerning therapy in all communities. People are beginning to embrace the idea of getting help instead of shunning those in need. It is my hope that this piece encourages at least one person to reach out and get the help they need.

EWhite2@MSP.edu

I want to end this chapter with a quick note on affirmations. If you don't know what an affirmation is, it is a formal declaration of a person.

Whether you realize it or not, you affirm yourself everyday with the thoughts you think and the words you speak.

So, how are you affirming yourself?

Growing up, my Mom always told me that "life and death is in the power of the tongue." When I was younger, I didn't exactly understand what that meant, but I do now more than ever.

Our life begins to take shape when we become intentional with every moment of our lives. Most importantly, the way we speak to *ourselves*. I became acquainted with reciting affirmations at the beginning of 2017. I was low on money and honestly just wanted to see if chanting "I AM A MONEY MAGNET" in the mirror over and over would magically bring me a few extra coins.

Well, it didn't.

What it did give me was the confidence to affirm myself into situations that did make me a money magnet. I now use affirmations everywhere: my vision boards, sticky notes on my bathroom mirror, in my car, the wallpaper to my cell phone, etc. This practice goes hand in hand with manifesting the things you want to see in your life. Manifesting doesn't just apply to material things, but feelings as well.

I've added a few of the affirmations I use daily below. Feel free to add your own and mix and match!

I HAVE THE POWER TO CONTROL MY THOUGHTS.

I WAS CREATED WHOLE. I AM MORE THAN ENOUGH.

I AM A MAGNET FOR SUPERNATURAL BLESSINGS.

I AM ATTRACTING MORE AND MORE MONEY INTO MY LIFE DAILY.

THE UNIVERSE IS ALWAYS CONSPIRING IN MY FAVOR.

I AM OVERFLOWING WITH LOVE, PEACE, ENERGY AND TIME.

MY MIND AND BODY ARE SOLID AND HEALTHY.

I RADIATE GOOD ENERGY AT ALL TIMES.

I HAVE SUPERNATURAL WEALTH, AND I GIVE GENEROUSLY AND ABUNDANTLY.

THE RELATIONSHIPS IN MY LIFE ARE STRONG AND HEALTHY.

I AM ATTRACTING WHO/WHAT NEEDS TO BE IN MY LIFE AT THIS VERY MOMENT.

GOD HAS GIVEN ME A SPIRIT OF LOVE, POWER, AND A SOUND MIND.

I AM BLESSED AND HIGHLY FAVORED AT ALL TIMES.

These are just a few that I recite to myself throughout the day. Give it a try and let me know how it works out for you!

PRO-TIP RECAP

PRO TIP #19 – SHOW GRATITUDE FOR YOUR LIFE

PRO TIP #20 – MIND YOUR MANNERS

PRO TIP #21 – TAKE CARE OF YOUR BODY. YOU ONLY GET ONE.

PRO TIP #22 – SELF-CARE IS MORE THAN MASSAGES

PRO TIP #23 – AFFIRM YOURSELF DAILY

Based off the tips in this chapter, how will you take control of your mental and emotional wellness? How will you use gratitude to attract the things you would like to see in your life?

1.)

2.)

3.)

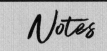

Notes

Notes

PRINCIPLE: VII

The World is Yours...
Explore It.

" Travel is never a matter of

money, but of courage."

–Paulo Coelho

I was 8 years old the first time I stepped foot on a plane.

My family and I were traveling to Disney World for my sister's 4th birthday. There are few experiences that I remember as a kid that have stuck with me, but that was definitely one of them. The concept of an airplane taking us from Detroit to an entirely new destination in just a few hours was wild to me. I still remember the way I felt as the plane took off and glided amongst a sea of fluffy white clouds, with the pristine blue sky peeking in between.

From that trip, I knew that I wanted to make travel a staple in my life.

I received my first passport in 2013 while still in undergrad at Georgia State. I applied for a study abroad program that the University had in place with CNN. As a budding journalist, I just knew that this experience would put me on the fast track to where I wanted to go in my career.

There was only one issue; I couldn't afford it.

The trip was roughly $5,500. I didn't have enough to pay for the passport fee of $150, so I knew that 5 Grand was out the window.

Something in my spirit told me that I should be on that trip though, so I did whatever I could to make it happen. I have a strong belief that nothing happens by chance, so it's by no surprise that I would soon run into my Fairy Godmother of Travel, Miss Paula Huntley.

Miss Huntley worked in the International Institute of Business at Georgia State, where she spearheaded the allocation of scholarship dollars to students seeking study abroad opportunities. I made an appointment with her and made the almost 40-minute trek to her office on foot.

During that initial meeting, she explained all of the scholarships and grants that I could apply for to fund the excursion. This instance is another prime example of pruning positive relationships with others. If it wasn't for Miss Huntley, I would've never been able to afford the trip, let alone a passport to board the plane. With her help, I became a Coca-Cola Global Ambassador Scholar, which meant that the company funded a large portion of my program's cost. By affording me this opportunity, I not only traveled abroad while earning school credit, but my vision expanded beyond belief. My mind was stretched in unimaginable ways, and my curiosity peaked. I wanted to learn more about the world around me every chance I could.

Students: Not only do you get school credit for studying abroad, it also looks **really, realllyyy** good on your resume.

At the time of this writing, in a 9-month span I've traveled to Israel, Dubai, Kenya, Russia and France (check out #Wheres-DaniGoing on Instagram.) Each experience was different, and I returned home with a sense of appreciation for my life and the people in it. I'd like to expound on the fact that each time you're introduced to a culturally rich experience such as travel, your view on your reality, your community, and even yourself will begin to change. I know that I gained a lot more empathy when I was exposed to the turmoil and tragedy that people just like us experience on a daily basis.

You don't have to go across the world to travel though.

Even if you've never been on a plane or out of your city, I believe that everyone owes it to themselves to experience something new out of their everyday life. That could mean taking a two-hour road trip or even a "staycation" in your own city. The power of travel and stepping out of my comfort zone to experience new things has enriched my life immensely. So much so, that I moved to an entirely new state all because I was experiencing a *beginning* life crisis.

I was 19 and dealing with my first heartbreak from a breakup with my high school sweetheart. For some reason, I thought that moving myself 700 miles from everything I knew would be the cure and I would automatically forget about him, and life would be peaches and cream all over again.

Well… that didn't happen, either.

A lot of good *did* happen, though. I was introduced to a new city, lifestyle and network, and I began to see a lot of personal growth within myself as well. When you're forced (or force yourself) into an entirely different environment, it's always tough at first because we're creatures of habit. Many of us like to stick to what we know. Typically, anything that may look out of the ordinary or poses a challenge is automatically out of the question for a lot of us.

My challenge to you is to push yourself past your boundaries and self-imposed limiting beliefs surrounding travel, experiences, and opportunities to better yourself. George Addair once said,

"Everything you've ever wanted is on the other side of fear."

Don't let a little temporary discomfort hold you back from living the life of your dreams.

PRO TIP 24

Move... you are not a tree! While this chapter was meant to be solely dedicated to travel, I believe this concept can be translated to all facets of life. Whether you're stuck in a dead-end job or relationship, or just wondering what your next move in life should be, I want to encourage you to always remain flexible. One of the best decisions I could've ever made was leaving everything that was familiar to me and moving to Atlanta 7 years ago. As fate would have it, I would not stay there forever, but the experiences that I had and the relationships that I cultivated will stick with me far beyond any measure of time. Open yourself up to welcoming new growth into your life through new experiences. You never know how your life will change because of one decision.

A QUICK NOTE ON PICKING UP AND MOVING: A few chapters ago I stated that a couple of weeks before my 23rd birthday, I received my first conditional offer letter to accept a position as a reporter in a tiny town 2 hours outside of Birmingham, Alabama. I had never heard of Dothan, AL. and to this day I do not know where it is on a map. My Dad drove me 16 hrs to that place in the middle of nowhere, (Remember, I still didn't have a license at this point) moved me into my apartment, slept on palettes with me on the floor because I didn't have furniture and dropped me off at work for my first two weeks in that unfamiliar place. (I'll never forget that. Thanks Dad!!) I would go on to sleep on that same palette in the middle of my apartment for 3 months after my Dad left to return home. In the words of street philosopher Kodak Black, "Sleeping on that palette, turned me to a savage." A new sense of motivation was awakened inside of me. Although this was not the most ideal time in my life, I know for a fact that if I had not made the decision to pack up and move to that unknown place, my life would not be what it is now. Please don't ever underestimate the power of ONE move changing your entire life. Sure, it was extremely uncomfortable, and I asked myself "what am I doing here?" several times a day, but it all worked out. Take that job, break up with that person, move across the country, whatever it is- just do it. If you're currently facing an uncomfortable/unfamiliar decision, PLEASE take the leap. Two things will happen: either you'll win, or you'll learn. Seems like a clear win/win to me.

HER STORY: Klaudia Jakubiak, Founder of The Travel Critic

To put it quite shortly, for many years, travel has been my therapy. In the moments of my life where I felt stuck, confused or unhappy, travel has always been my cure. Travel allows me to step outside of my daily mundane thoughts and anxieties, and revitalizes me to feel, see and experience the unknown; pushing me to uncomfortable and unfamiliar places. Whether it's jumping on the backseat of locals' scooters in Bali or expanding my taste palette in Ho Chi Minh, travel has enriched my life in ways that I couldn't imagine. The further I've traveled into the unknown, the closer I've come to my own truth. The experiences I've faced in my travels have shaped me into someone that I'm proud of, but the journey wasn't easy...

After working in the corporate world for over six years, I felt burnt out and dealing with a lack luster of life. I was lost. I really didn't know which direction to go, but a voice in the back of my head was constantly telling me to take a jump. So, I did. I booked a one-way ticket to Vietnam. Without a plan or itinerary for Southeast Asia, I was guided by my intuition to explore a place completely foreign to me. Naturally, many of my friends were curious of how I was able to 'pull off such a thing'. It didn't require much money, but it did require a whole lot of faith.

So, you might be wondering how much money was required to do such a thing? I purposely chose Southeast Asia because it is really affordable. There was definitely some strategy involved; for instance, hotels/hostels cost anywhere from $10 - $50 per night. And food? Well, you can practically eat like a king or queen for $20 per day. I knew the most expensive part of my trip was the flight to get there. I saved up all my credit card points to use for the flight, so technically I only needed money for accommodations and food. The number one piece of advice I have for longer-term travel is to book hostels. Many people make a sour face when they hear the word "hostel" but truly, they will not only help you save money but also connect with incredible like-minded people. The hostels in Southeast Asia never exceeded $20 per night, and some of them included pools and felt more like villas! Additionally, you're more likely to be exploring the cities and immersing yourself in culture, so spending a lot of money on accommodations is a waste. In comparison, I experienced 5-star resorts and yes, I was experiencing a luxurious stay, but I did not feel connected. While staying in hostels, I was instantly connected with likeminded individuals from all over the world. I created friendships based on interests and organic connections... something that I never experienced while staying in luxury resorts.

The journey through self-development is never-ending but I have found my vessel that helps me understand the world better, and more importantly myself. If you are deciding whether or not to take the jump, just trust your gut, because you never know what is on the receiving end, and that's the beauty of this life.

IG: @TheTravelCritic I www.thetravelcritic.com

PRO TIP 25

Discovering yourself through travel. At this point in my life, I've lived in 3 different states and traveled to 7 different countries. The most intense growth I've ever experienced was a direct result of picking up and navigating my way through a new place. One of the best gifts that you can ever give yourself is experiencing life through a global lens. From serving as keynote at one of the top technology summits in Moscow, Russia to living in Dothan, Alabama for 6 months during my first TV News stint. Whether the experience was amazing or horrible, it all aided in my growth, and I'm positive stepping out of your 'travel' comforts will do the same for you!

Based off the tips in this chapter, how will you discover yourself through travel? What 3 places do you plan to visit (or move to) this year?

1.)

2.)

3.)

Notes

Notes

Epilogue

While reading Dani's book, I couldn't help but think what the perception would be of how she was raised. Surely, I instilled, with persistence the importance of making your bed every day and the feeling of peace and serenity you find with you enter a room with a made bed. I must have stressed this time and time again ever since Dani was old enough to pull a sheet over a bed. Certainly no one would have such a penchant for making sure this ritual was done each and every morning without a Mom hot on your heels when it wasn't done.

Well, I was not that Mom.

I never made Dani or her sister make their beds, and most times I hurried out of the house without making my own bed! I was not that Mom. However, I was that Mom who instilled in my kids a made-up mind when it came to having a love and passion for God and a close relationship with Him. I was that Mom who made it my business to be their cheerleader each and every time they needed a kind word and a shoulder to cry on. I was that Mom who inspired them to have a love of self and knowledge that you can do anything you put your mind to.

So, in being that Mom, I raised a God-fearing independent daughter with drive, determination, and dreams. The drive to have her own non-profit, the determination to have book sales out of this world, and a made-up bed to enter for her sweet dreams.

It is my hope that after reading this book you've received some priceless inspiration to aid you on your journey through life. I hope that you'll take the transparency in these pages and create a life that you will be proud of. I've always told my daughter that it doesn't matter how you begin the race, what matters is how you finish it.

In the words of my late father, "The race is not won by the swift, but, (s)he who endures unto the end.

Wherever you currently find yourself in life, endure unto the end. Everything gets greater later.

Wishing you all of God's best!

-Ingrid Ellis

(One proud mama)

About the Author

DANIELLE D. HUGHES

"I believe that this work is needed to show our young people that no matter their circumstance, they can become whatever they desire." -Danielle D. Hughes

With reverberating purpose and strategic strides, Danielle D. Hughes has become one of Detroit's most recognizable millennials for youth advocacy and empowerment. Pledging daily to be the person she says she needed when she was younger, the astute social entrepreneur, humanitarian and proud Detroit, MI native, makes it her mission to make an impact in the lives of her hometown youth by providing teens with mentorship, coaching, leadership and personal development skills to achieve their dreams.

Named to Forbes '30 under '30 2018 list for her profound work in education, Danielle is a striking example of dreams realized, creatively directing and hosting her own vision board series in cities across the country since 2015.

Through her pivotal actions exposing young people in

low-income communities to life-enhancing opportunities, Danielle has been honored as one of 25 of the most powerful women in Detroit by Walkers Legacy and Woman Of The Year by the Zeta Nu Zeta Chapter of Zeta Phi Beta Sorority, Inc, Vanguard Award recipient by the Detroit Young Professionals, named a 'Leader of Tomorrow' by the Native Detroiter Magazine, a Top 30 under 40 by M-Lifestyle and the esteemed honor of being one of the most influential African Americans by The Root. Coupling her youth advocacy with contributions to women empowerment campaigns, Danielle believes fearlessness, grace, tenacity and unapologetic excellence is what makes herself and women alike, powerful.

Danielle holds a B.A. in Journalism from Georgia State University. Noting her triple threat for success and serenity, she is an unwavering lover of God, good novels and good manners.

Made in the USA
Middletown, DE
20 July 2019